Hotel/Motel
Front Desk Personnel

(Courtesy Holiday Inns, Inc.)

HOTEL/MOTEL
FRONT DESK PERSONNEL

GRACE PAIGE

JANE PAIGE

VNR **Van Nostrand Reinhold**
_____New York

First published in the U.K. by Cassell Ltd, 1977, under the title *The Hotel Receptionist*
Second edition, 1984
First American edition published in 1989 by Van Nostrand Reinhold

Library of Congress Catalog Card Number 88-12664
ISBN 0-442-20491-4

Printed in the United States of America
Designed by Sharon Lawburgh

Van Nostrand Reinhold
115 Fifth Avenue
New York, New York 10003

Van Nostrand Reinhold (International) Limited
11 New Fetter Lane
London EC4P 4EE, England

Van Nostrand Reinhold
480 La Trobe Street
Melbourne, Victoria 3000, Australia

Macmillan of Canada
Division of Canada Publishing Corporation
164 Commander Boulevard
Agincourt, Ontario M1S 3C7, Canada

16 15 14 13 12 11 10 9 8 7 6 5 4 3 2 1

Library of Congress Cataloging-in-Publication Data

Paige, Grace.
    Hotel/motel front desk personnel / Grace Paige, Jane Paige.
        p. cm.
    Bibliography: p.
    Includes index.
    ISBN 0-442-20491-4 (pbk.)
    1. Hotel management.   2. Motel management.   I. Paige, Jane.
    II. Title
    TX911.3.M27P35 1989
    647'.94'068–dc19   88-12664
                                                            CIP

To "Jim"
whose love, devotion, and patience
make our work possible

Contents

5 BOOKKEEPING AND ACCOUNTING   99

Preface

The rapid expansion of the hotel and tourism industry during the past two decades has been phenomenal, and modern microcomputer technology has revolutionized front office procedures. However, the basic principles underlying good hotel reception and front office disciplines will still be applicable whether a public lodging establishment has the latest computerized equipment or is manually operated.

Even the most sophisticated computers have been known to fail; therefore, it is essential for front office personnel to have an understanding of manually operated systems and be able to carry out the necessary tasks without any interruption to the flow of business.

After many years teaching courses on hotel management and the principles and practices of front office reception, we discovered upon a review of course critiques that while the courses and the lectures were rated "good" and "interesting" the textbooks were rated only "average."

The main criticisms of the texts focussed on the following points: that most of the authors presumed that the students have prior knowledge, that the language was too academic, and that there was a lack of illustrative diagrams and practical instruction to positively reinforce the learning experience.

We decided that a new kind of text for front office personnel could be written that would overcome these faults. It has been a challenge to write a clear, concise, and easily understood text which covers all aspects of front office procedures from bottom to top and which is suitable for students enrolled in two- or four-year programs in hotel administration and related subjects (such as hotel and motel management and front office reception procedures and practices) but we believe the results have been worth the effort.

It is also hoped that this text will be a useful reference book for trainees and other people comparatively new to the hospitality industry.

SPECIAL FEATURES

The history of the growth of an industry always captures the imagination, and chapter 1 describes briefly how the hospitality business in the United States developed from the days of the stagecoach stopovers into an international industry grossing billions of dollars annually.

Chapter 2 highlights the social skills and desirable qualities for those who aspire to be first class front desk personnel. But the charming, well-spoken person who greets the arriving guest is only one aspect of the job requirement. The innumerable tasks and functions dealt with in chapter 3 illustrate that the job also requires trained, capable, intelligent people if the office is to run smoothly.

The hospitality industry is highly competitive and if the hotel/motel is to achieve its goal of maximum occupancy and profitability, the product, which is the hotel and its facilities, must be marketed and sold succuessfully. Chapter 4 emphasizes that front desk personnel must have a thorough knowledge of their product as they are an important part of the sales and marketing team.

Chapters 5 and 6 give the basic principles underlying the double-entry bookkeeping system and business practice. A general knowledge of these subjects is essential for all front office personnel before they specialize in any one area of reception work.

Reports and statistics are the tools of management from which decisions are made. Chapter 7 aquaints the students with some of the basic reports and statistics that are necessary to assist managerial decisions.

It is not possible in this text to go into detail regarding the legal aspects which relate to the hotel industry, but chapter 8 presents a broad overview. It is essential that front office personnel have a knowledge of the basic rules and regulations governing hotels and restaurants in order to handle any problems that may arise during the course of their duties and responsibilities.

The chapter quiz at the end of each chapter is intended to consolidate the learning experience, and the topics for discussion are designed to motivate research and group discussion.

Acknowledgments

We wish to thank the following for their cooperation:

The American Automobile Association (AAA)
American Express Travel Related Services Company, Inc.
AT&T Information Systems
Citicorp Diners Club, Inc.
Holiday Inns, Inc.—Hotel Group
Marriott Corporation
MasterCard International Incorporated
NCR Corporation
Sweda International
VISA, U.S.A., Inc.
Whitney Duplicating Check Company
Xerox Corporation
The Florida Department of Commerce/Division of
    Economic Development/Bureau of Economic
    Analysis/Division of Tourism
The Florida Hotel & Motel Association
U.S. Department of Labor
Equal Employment Opportunity Commission
City of Sarasota, Florida
State of Florida Department of Business Regulation,
    Division of Hotels and Restaurants

INTRODUCTION

THE HISTORY OF THE INDUSTRY

Inns have been in existence since ancient times. The establishment of money as a unit of exchange, in about the sixth century B.C., gave people the impetus to trade and travel. As horizons widened, the demand for food and lodgings for the traveler increased, and many people turned their private dwelling places into lodging houses where a weary traveler could rest and partake of a meal.

The early inns were neither clean nor sanitary, and landlords gained a reputation for being disreputable and dishonest. The emergence of the public lodging establishment as a significant commercial institution began in the early 1700s after the Industrial Revolution in Great Britain. The roadside inns of England, which gained a reputation as being the finest in the world, had a character all their own.

During colonial times in the U.S., hotels were usually located around seaports, but when stagecoaches started carrying passengers across the continent, inns and taverns began to be constructed along the stagecoach routes.

In 1794 the City Hotel, the first building in America to be designed specifically as a hotel, opened in New York. It had seventy-three rooms and soon became a social center of the city. Not to be outdone, Baltimore followed with its own City Hotel, Boston with the Exchange Coffee House, and Philadelphia with the Mansion House; these also became fashionable meeting places.

In 1829 the opening of the luxurious Tremont House in Boston established America's supremacy over European hotels. Its architect Isaiah Rogers became the leading consultant on hotel construction, and his influence dominated the field for some fifty years.

In the next century competition was fierce in the hotel construction business, every major city claiming to have the finest hotels in the country: Chicago's Grand Pacific, Palmer House, and Sherman; San Francisco's Palace; Denver's Brown Palace; and New York's Waldorf Astoria. These hotels catered to a rich and famous clientele.

By the 1900s as travel became easier and less expensive a more affluent middle-class American society joined commercial travelers in traveling for pleasure and business. The enterprising Ellsworth M. Statler foresaw this new trend, and on 18 January 1908, the opening of the Buffalo Statler, a commercial hotel, marked the beginning of a new era in the growth of the hospitality industry. Statler's slogan was "A Room and Bath for a Dollar and a Half."

During the 1920s the construction of new hotels reached a peak. Professional schools of hotel management were created, along with technical schools for the training of chefs and other skilled hotel workers. There was also a significant trend towards corporate rather than private ownership of hotels because of rising building and operating costs.

This was a golden age for the industry, but it did not last long. The Great Depression of the 1930s brought hotel construction and expansion almost to a standstill. It was not until World War II that the hotel industry recovered, thanks to a mass movement of servicemen and others engaged in the war effort. New areas were chosen for defense plants making it necessary for people to relocate or travel. There was a tremendous new demand for lodgings. Hotel accommodation was at a premium with hotel occupancy running at over 90 percent, but standards declined as many trained, skilled hotel workers were drafted into the armed services.

The 1950s saw a new trend and a different type of accommodation becoming popular. Mr. and Mrs. America were on the move in the family automobile and "motels" began to boom. Established hoteliers recognized that this new phenomenon was here to stay and began to incorporate the motel into their businesses.

Another major development that began in the 1950s was the franchise system. Research proved that travelers react to brand names and brand identification symbols. Under the franchise system one can go into business for oneself and at the same time receive the benefits of being associated with a well-known group or chain of hotels/motels.

It is a legal, business, and personal relationship, and as with any partnership agreement, both sides have expectations and specific concrete obligations to each other.

A franchisee must pay an initial fee and a portion of the gross receipts to the franchisor. In return the franchisor offers his trademark, operational system, concept, and many other support services such as advertising, marketing, and training programs.

THE HOSPITALITY INDUSTRY TODAY

In today's shrinking, fast-moving world, airlines, passenger ships, trains, buses, and automobiles carry travelers all over the globe on either pleasure or business trips. These travelers require food, lodgings, and service of a good standard and at a reasonable price.

In every state, new hotels offer improved standards of accommodation, restaurants, bars, banquet halls, and facilities for meetings, conventions, and recreation. The United States is the tourist capital of the world, and the dollar value of travel grosses billions for the industry every year.

Hotel management today is controlled by computers and data processors which spew out a continuous stream of information on unit costs, budgets, payroll control systems, market research analysis, and statistics. Progressive and enterprising analysts study the latest trends and developments endeavoring to anticipate future trends.

It is a fiercely competitive business; every operator aims for maximum occupancy and profitability. This goal is achieved by improving efficiency within the establishment and by offering the highest standard of accommodation, facilities, and service at competitive prices.

The phenomenal growth and expansion of the industry since the 1960s has created a constant demand for trained, skilled staff. With modern management and new business techniques the future will bring an increasing demand for intelligent, well-educated young people trained in science and technology. Hotel management provides ample career opportunities for those temperamentally suited to the job.

DIFFERENT TYPES OF PUBLIC
LODGING ESTABLISHMENTS

Public lodging establishments fall into many different categories ranging from large hotels and motels, to small country inns, cottages, and ranches, to resort complexes and apartments.

The type of guest to whom the establishment caters gives it special characteristics and atmosphere. Airport hotels, for example, usually cater to travelers making brief stopovers while still in transit. The resort hotels, which are seasonal, cater to the vacationer; many off-set their low-season lulls by offering special rates and providing facilities for conventions, conferences, trade fairs, meetings, seminars, and other special events.

Many motoring organizations, such as the American Automobile Association (AAA), make their own classification of public lodging and catering establishments to assist the traveler in choosing accommodation. Their field representatives inspect and screen each facility against the group's standards. In addition to providing an indication as to the type of establishment, each facility is also rated for quality.

Terms Used in AAA Listings
(©AAA—Reproduced by Permission)

Types of lodging
Motel
Hotel
Suites
Lodge
Historical
Ranch
Apartment
Motor Inn
Motor Hotel
Cottages
Country Inns
Complex
Resort

The AAA Diamonds
(©AAA—Reproduced by Permission)

◆   Meets AAA basic requirements for recommendation.
◆◆   Exceeds AAA minimum requirements in some physical and/or operational categories.
◆◆◆   Significantly exceeds AAA requirements in many physical and

operational categories. Offers very comfortable and attractive accommodations.

♦♦♦ Exceptional; significantly exceeds in most physical and operational categories. Offers luxurious accommodations as well as extra amenities. The management, staff, housekeeping, and maintenance rank well above the average.

♦♦♦♦ Renowned: awarded only to those exceptional properties that are widely recognized for marked superiority of guest facilities, services, and overall atmosphere.

HOTEL ORGANIZATION

Organization means the arrangement of personnel and the assignment of their duties and responsibilities so that the establishment functions as one unit. It is important that there are clear lines of authority and of communications.

The organization of the establishment will depend on its size and type. In a small hotel (fig. 1-1) the organization is comparatively simple, with a manager supervising all areas of operation. Communications should be direct and easy, and the personnel should be able to relate their work to that of other departments.

In medium-size hotels the tasks must be subdivided into separate work areas and supervised by section supervisors. In very large hotels (fig. 1-2) the volume of work is such that under departmental heads the staff often specialize in only one aspect of the work, and there is little opportunity to relate their individual efforts to the whole operation.

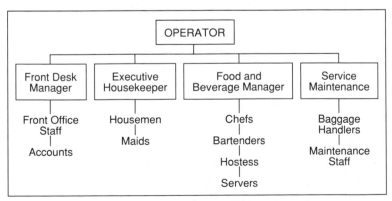

1-1. Organization of a small inn or motel.

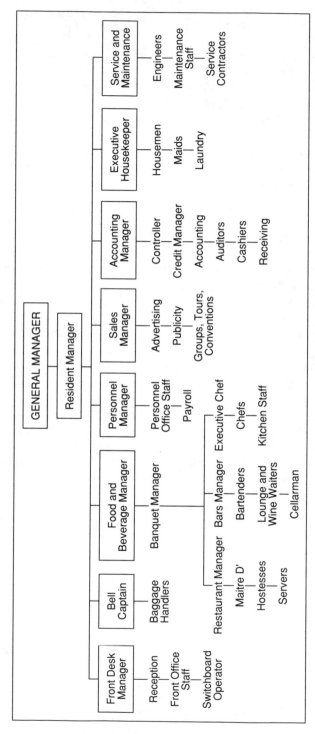

1-2. Organization of a large hotel.

DIFFERENT TYPES OF ROOM ACCOMMODATION

The large hotel and motel groups often standardize their rooms so that the descriptive types of accommodation offered have the same basic facilities whatever the size or location of the establishment.

STANDARD. One or two double beds, a dresser, and a work area

KING LEISURE. King-size bed, large work area, sofa or sofa bed, or two easy chairs

KING. Room with a king-size bed

QUEEN-de-Luxe. Room with two queen-size beds

QUEEN. Room with one queen-size bed

EXECUTIVE. One bed and one sofa bed

STUDIO. Two single sofa beds

SUITE. One or two bedrooms and a living room

PARLOR. Living room with one double bed

KITCHENETTE. Room with kitchen unit

TERMS AND ABBREVIATIONS

Hotel directories and guidebooks use symbols and abbreviations to describe their listings. It is important that front desk personnel familiarize themselves with the terms and abbreviations used.

Terms (©AAA—Reproduced by Permission)

A/C. Air conditioning.

Airport Transp. Provided to and from the establishment. There may be a charge.

Cooking Facilities. The word *kitchen* denotes the presence of full cooking equipment. The word *efficiency* denotes complete or less-than-complete cooking equipment within the sleeping room.

Credit Cards. AE (American Express), CB (Carte Blanche), DI (Diners Club), MC (MasterCard), VI (Visa).

Meal Plans. Rates quoted for EP (European plan, without meals); AP (American plan, three meals); MAP (Modified American Plan, two meals); BP (breakfast plan, full breakfast); CP (continental plan, breakfast of pastry, juice, and other beverages).

Movies. In-room movies at a charge or sometimes in-house movies free of charge.

⬛ Wheelchair traveler accommodations providing facilities for wheelchair travelers.

Nonsmoking symbol. Nonsmokers' rooms are available at lodgings whose listings carry the symbol ⊗.

Pets. "Pets" or "No Pets" used when applicable. By law, pet restrictions do not apply to guide dogs accompanying blind persons in the United States.

Smoke Detectors. Denoted by symbol D.

Sprinkler Systems. Denoted by symbol S.

Television. Televisions in rooms are designated by C/TV (color TV), CATV (cable TV), or C/CATV (color cable TV).

WKends. Friday and Saturday nights.

Other Abbreviations

Add'l. Additional.
Adj. Adjacent.
Banq. Banquet.
Conv. Convention.
Ctr. Center.
Enter. Entertainment.
Free trans. Free transportation.
HBO. Free-in-room Home Box Office movies.
Htd. pool. Heated pool.
Hwy. Highway.
Jct. Junction.
Min. Minimum.
Mtgs. Meetings.
Ngt. Night.
Opp. Opposite.
Pk. Park.
RB. Rollaway bed charge.
Rest. Restaurant.
Sp. Special event when a rate increase and/or minimum stay and/or advance deposit apply.
XP. Third or fourth person charge.

THE FUNCTION OF THE RECEPTION OFFICE

In all hospitality establishments, the front desk is the focal point. Front office personnel are expected to be charming, tactful, diplomatic, and capable of dealing with the public as well as carrying out the innumerable tasks that ensure the smooth and efficient running of the front-of-house operations.

Whether it is a small inn or a large hotel with clearly defined areas for advance reservations, cashier, billing, accounts, switchboard, and front desk reception, the function of the front office is to:

1. Sell accommodation
2. Receive and welcome guests
3. Check-in and register guests
4. Check-out guests and deal with the settlement of accounts
5. Provide information and handle inquiries or complaints
6. Deal with advance reservations
7. Chart all reservations
8. Keep up-to-the-minute records of room status
9. Handle incoming and outgoing mail
10. Deal with telephone communications
11. Attend to all photocopying
12. Maintain good communications with all other departments

The Front Office Manager

The main responsibilities of the front office manager are to:

1. Have a knowledge of all the front desk duties, be able to develop an effective team, and supervise and maintain a smoothly running shift
2. Serve as a role model by demonstrating effective guest relations, handling guest problems and complaints
3. Know corporate, federal, state, and local regulations pertaining to the operation of the establishment
4. Know about the other departments within the hotel and how each affects the front office, and ensure good communications with all departments
5. Orient, train, counsel, and evaluate all employees in the front office. Prepare employee schedules and be knowledgeable of benefits programs and policies pertaining to the Equal Employment Opportunity Commission (EEOC), the Equal Pay Act (EPA), the Age Discrimination in Employment Act (ADEA), the Pregnancy Discrimination Act (PDA), guarantee of fair treatment, and termination
6. Know emergency procedures; investigate and report guest

and employee accidents and ensure front office personnel are aware of all property and safety precautions

7. Know how to operate front office equipment and how to report malfunctions
8. Be able to conduct quality control and audits, enforce credit procedures, and monitor selling procedures; know the duties and responsibilities of the night audit staff
9. Understand operating statements, budget worksheets, and other financial reports; be able to adhere to budget commitments in sales, average room rates, occupancy, work schedules, and wages
10. Speak clearly and concisely, write effectively, listen attentively, and keep staff informed of all pertinent information

The Billing Office

This section of the front office concentrates on the recording of all daily sales, creating guests' folios (bills), and ensuring that all charges are posted to the correct account. Computerized, automatic billing is used in large hotels; billing machines, and sometimes manual billing and tabular ledger systems, are used in smaller establishments.

Whatever system is used, posting charges to accounts must be kept up-to-the-minute so that it is possible to produce a guest's bill immediately upon request.

The Cashier's Office

The cashier's office handles all payments of guests' accounts, deals with credit card verification, cashes checks and traveler's checks, and sees to petty cash disbursements, safety deposit boxes, and placement of valuables in the hotel safe.

The Information Desk

The room key and letter or message racks are usually located at the information desk, and there the staff handle all inquiries and messages.

The Bell Captain's Desk

The bell captain is responsible for the supervision and assignment of duties to the front-of-house uniformed staff. In large hotels the bell captain's desk not only deals with guests' baggage, but also arranges taxi service, theater tickets, tour reservations, and general inquiries about events, local entertainment, and places of interest.

The Housekeeping Department

Under the supervision of an executive housekeeper, this department is responsible for maintaining the guest rooms and public rooms in a clean sanitary condition. It is essential that there is direct communication and liaison between the front office and the housekeeping department. In order to sell accommodation efficiently the front desk must know the room status at all times.

Restaurants, Bars, and Kitchen

The food and beverage manager, restaurant manager, bars manager, and executive chef are responsible for the organization and smooth running of their respective departments. Each must ensure that there are always good communications and liaison with other departments, particularly with the front office.

CHAPTER SUMMARY

This chapter briefly traces the history of the public lodging establishment and describes the functions of the front office.
Important points discussed are:

- Different types of public lodging establishments
- The information provided to the traveler by motoring and other organizations
- The importance of hotel organization, clear lines of authority, and good lines of communication
- The types of room accommodation offered to the traveler

- The language of the hotel business, the terms and abbreviations used
- The function of the front office and the role of the front office manager
- The subdivision of the front office into different sections each dealing with specific tasks

FOR DISCUSSION

1. Discuss how and why the public lodging establishment has developed into the modern hotel business, offering every type of service and facility.
2. Research and list the different types of public lodging establishments in your area and describe the accommodations and facilities they offer.
3. Discuss the trends and social behavior patterns that could have an effect on the hospitality industry.
4. The economic state of a country can have a profound effect on the hospitality industry. Discuss the effect of (a) an economic recession, (b) an economic boom.

KEY TERMS

Public lodging establishment
Hotel operator
AAA diamonds
Hotel organization
Standardized accommodation
Corporate, federal, state, and local regulations
Market research analysis
Maximum occupancy
Profitability

CHAPTER QUIZ

1. Describe briefly five different categories of public lodging establishments and the type of accommodation and facilities they could offer.

2. What are the basic principles of good hotel organization?

3. What is the basic function of the front office? Enumerate its responsibilities.

4. Write a job description for the function of a front office manager.

5. Write briefly on why good communication and liaison between the front office and other departments are so important in a hotel.

6. What do the following terms and abbreviations mean?
    a. ♦♦♦ (AAA)
    b. Accommodation
        1. King Leisure 2. Standard 3. Queen de luxe 4. Studio 5. Suite.
    c. Credit Cards
        1. AE 2. DI 3. MC 4. CB 5. V
    d. Meal Plans.
        1. MAP 2. CP 3. AP 4. BP 5. EP
    e. Other Abbreviations
        1. CCATV 2. Banq. 3. HBO 4. Conv. 5. RB 6. SP 7. Enter. 8. XP 9. D and S 10. Mtgs.

2

SOCIAL SKILLS

THE ROLE OF FRONT DESK RECEPTION PERSONNEL

The front office is the nerve center of the hotel. Not only is it the communication center for the servicing departments, but it is also both the first and last point of contact for guests. Therefore, front desk reception personnel play a special role in the establishment.

Many qualities are desirable in first-class front desk personnel. Some of these qualities, such as charm and personality, come naturally; others can be acquired by good training and the conscious development of social skills and personal attributes.

A smile of welcome from a charming, attractive, well-groomed, well-spoken associate at reception immediately creates a warm, friendly atmosphere for the traveler on arrival. It is equally important that the person be capable, competent, and intelligent, to ensure that the many tasks and functions of the office are carried out efficiently and smoothly.

POISE AND DEPORTMENT

The term *poise* is difficult to define. It is the self-discipline that enables one to appear serenely dignified despite headache, weary feet, or confrontations with an irate guest. Poise is the ability to be friendly yet businesslike, to suggest efficiency without frenzied effort, to be self-assured without appearing smug or patronizing.

15

Poise is directly concerned with good deportment, with how you walk and carry yourself. A brisk step indicates that you are interested in your job. Never slouch along, drooping your shoulders; never flop awkwardly in a chair. Aim for neat foot and hand movements and a graceful carriage. Remember, poise and good deportment can be cultivated, and achieving them will give a sense of well-being and an improved mental attitude. You can never feel good about yourself and completely at ease if you are self-conscious about your appearance and movements.

PERSONAL APPEARANCE AND HYGIENE

Anyone who has to deal with the public or who is in continual contact with other people as part of their job must always be aware that attention to their appearance and personal hygiene is of utmost importance. It does not take much imagination to realize the bad impression that can be created by an unkempt appearance. The front desk associate should appear on duty immaculate in every way.

While styles and trends change, there are certain basic principles that remain the same. Here are some tips for following those principles.

Hair

Extremes in hair styles are not advocated while on duty. Neat, clean hair, cut or arranged in a style that keeps it out of the way of the work area is best.

Makeup

There is no lack of advice on the use of makeup, and a little makeup is fine. It should never be heavily applied. Good eating habits, a nutritional diet, exercise, and a reasonable amount of sleep all lend themselves to good health, which in return will be reflected in a clear complexion, bright eyes, and a healthy body which are attractive in themselves.

Hands

Hands are always on display. Pay close attention to their appearance. Female personnel should choose a subdued nail polish, if they wear it. Both men's and women's nails should be well manicured.

Clothing

Many establishments provide uniforms for the staff to wear when on duty. In this case, it only takes keeping them fresh and crisp to look your best. If the choice of clothing is left to you, avoid extremes in high fashion. Opt instead for classic, conservative styles. Women should keep a spare pair of stockings or pantyhose handy in case of runs. Shoes should be neat but comfortable as a great deal of time is spent standing.

Halitosis

Halitosis (bad breath) can be unpleasant and create a bad impression. The causes are numerous, but sensible diet and regular brushing and flossing will help. One should visit the dentist for regular check-ups and cleaning, and if the problem persists, a visit to a doctor may be necessary to determine the cause.

Body Odor

Like halitosis, body odor can be extremely unpleasant and embarrassing. Reception personnel should make every effort to shower regularly and use a good deodorant. It is very important that a guest's first contact with hotel personnel be a pleasant one.

VOICE AND SPEECH

Front desk personnel are in constant oral communication with the public; therefore, one's voice must be pleasing and manner of speech correct. Clear enunciation is very important, particularly when speaking into the telephone. Avoid slangy expressions. Listen to a tape recording of your voice, note the defects, and consciously practice both enunciation and correct pronunciation.

TELEPHONE MANNER

It is essential that all front office personnel develop a telephone personality. Whether in taking a reservation or answering an inquiry, remember that you cannot be seen, only heard and that the image you project over the telephone will reflect the image of the hotel. The voice should be well modulated, the spoken words clear and distinct, and the tone friendly, interested, and helpful. Never sound mechanical, indifferent, or impatient.

The following simple rules will help to develop a good telephone manner and technique:

1. Answer the telephone promptly. Always have a pencil and notepad by you—being kept waiting and having to repeat things will make the caller impatient.
2. Greet the caller pleasantly with, for example, "Peacock Lodge, this is Jane, may I help you?" Never say, "Hi! this is Jane." If it is an internal call, answer, "Reception desk, this is Jane, may I help you?"
3. Callers usually respond by giving their name and stating their business, but if they do not, ask tactfully, "May I ask who is calling please?" or "May I help you?"
4. Listen attentively, and if information or details have to be recorded, write them down clearly and legibly, as they are given, then repeat them back to the caller to ensure that you have the correct information.
5. If a message has to be taken, be certain to record the date and time of message, who it is for, and who it is from, and always repeat the message back to the caller to ensure that all the details are correct.
6. When receiving incoming calls for executives or management, always ascertain who the caller is and, if possible, the nature of his or her business, then check to see whether the member of staff wishes to accept the call. Busy executives should not be bothered by trifling matters, so any member of staff taking an incoming call must learn how to classify and route them to the person best suited to deal with the caller.

The following two examples will demonstrate effective telephone manner.

Example 1
Reception: Peacock Lodge, this is Jane, may I help you?
Caller: May I speak to the manager?
Reception: May I ask who is calling?
Caller: Mrs. Jones, I have a reservation for July 30 and I would like a word with your manager.

Reception: (Quickly checking the advance booking chart) Yes, Mrs. Jones, we have a room reserved for you, can I be of any assistance?

Caller: Well I just wanted to ask the manager if it is alright to bring my poodle with me?

Reception: That will be quite alright Mrs. Jones. Peacock Lodge does have facilities for small pets at a charge of $1.25 a day, but I'm sorry they are not allowed in the restaurants or lounges. Would you like me to make arrangements for your poodle?

Caller: Yes, please.

In this example, the clerk has tactfully ascertained the nature of the call, realized that it could be handled without bothering a busy manager, dealt with the inquiry, and reassured the caller, thus establishing a good relationship.

Example 2

Reception: Peacock Lodge, this is Jane, may I help you?

Caller: This is Bill Jones, president of the Sidham Sailing Club. I want to discuss the seating arrangement for our annual dinner on November 30.

Reception: Good morning, Mr. Jones. If you will please hold, I will put you through to Mr. Wyatt our assistant manager for special functions.

In this example, the reception associate will then locate Mr. Wyatt and inform him that Mr. Jones, president of the Sidham Sailing Club, is on the line, wishing to talk about the seating arrangements for their annual dinner. This will alert Mr. Wyatt of the nature of the call.

There is nothing more irritating to a caller than to be put on hold and be kept waiting, so if it takes any time at all to locate Mr. Wyatt the reception associate should go back quickly to the caller and ask for a telephone number so that Mr. Wyatt can return the call, making sure Mr. Wyatt gets the message to return Mr. Jones's call.

TACT AND DIPLOMACY

Diplomacy is the art of conducting negotiations between people. Tact is the skill of handling a difficult person or situation without giving offense.

The day-to-day experience of dealing with people and problems will develop the skills of tact and diplomacy. It is not difficult to deal with people who are pleasant and cooperative, but it requires intelligence, understanding, patience, common sense, and self-discipline to handle difficult, awkward people or situations without giving offense and without putting yourself or the management in the wrong.

The following examples illustrate the type of situation that could call for the utmost tact and diplomacy.

Example 1

Guests in the hotel restaurant have already complained without satisfaction to the waiter about the dinner they have been served, so they have descended on the reception desk demanding to see the manager. The manager is not available and the reception associate on duty is confronted with handling the immediate problem.

In this situation it is absolutely essential that the reception associate remain cool, calm, and in control. The exact cause of the complaint should be ascertained. The restaurant manager and executive chef must be contacted immediately. The guests must be persuaded gently to return to the restaurant where they will be served with another, more satisfactory meal and be offered a complimentary drink.

As you can imagine, in this situation, the reception associate will require patience, self-control, initiative, resourcefulness, understanding, and persuasiveness.

Example 2

Mr. Green, a guest at the hotel, is dining in the restaurant with a very attractive young woman, when another woman arrives at the reception desk and announces that she is Mr. Green's wife and asks that he be paged immediately.

To avoid any possible embarrassment the reception associate should ask Mrs. Green to take a seat in the reception area. She should then telephone to the restaurant manager who will be asked to inform Mr. Green discreetly that his wife wishes to speak to him at the reception desk. If the public address system has to be used to page Mr. Green, the words for the announcement should be carefully chosen, for example: "Will Mr. Green please come to the reception desk," not "Mr. Green, your wife is waiting at the reception desk."

Example 3

An urgent message is received for Mrs. Carter, one of the guests. The caller asks if Mrs. Carter can be informed as gently as possible that a very close relative has died. The hotel manager is not available, nor is the front office manager, and the reception associate has been asked to cope with the situation until they get back. In a situation like this, it would be advisable to use the privacy of the manager's office, order a pot of coffee, and have a drink of brandy or something similar handy. Then send a message to Mrs. Carter making sure it does not alarm her, asking if she could call at the manager's office as soon as possible. On her arrival, invite her to sit down and offer her a cup of coffee. Then as gently as possible, break the news, and offer every possible assistance for any arrangements she may have to make.

Example 4
A guest complains to the reception desk that she has no soap or clean towels in her room and that it has obviously not been cleaned that day. The reception associate will ascertain the name and room number of the guest, apologize for the oversight, and reassure her that the matter will be dealt with immediately. The reception office will contact the executive housekeeper at once, inform him or her of the complaint, and get an assurance that the room will be serviced at once.

In general, when dealing with any kind of complaint made by a guest:

1. The name and room number of the person making the complaint should be recorded.
2. The exact nature of the complaint should be noted.
3. The guest must be reassured that the complaint, no matter how trivial, will be dealt with immediately.
4. The complaint should be followed up by contacting the supervisor of the area concerned, who should take action.

DEALING WITH VERBAL INQUIRIES

Inquiries made in person at the front desk should be dealt with quickly and efficiently to prevent lines from forming. The reception associate must learn how to extract the exact nature of information required in order to classify the inquiry. The reception office should be so well organized that all sources of information necessary to answer any likely inquiry from guests or others are at hand. The layout of the hotel, the facilities, the organization, and the names of all supervisors in the servicing departments should be memorized, so that any inquiries, complaints, or calls concerning them can be routed to the person best suited to deal with them.

TYPES OF INQUIRIES

Reservations

To deal with inquiries about reservations, the reception associate must have on hand up-to-the-minute information of room status, the advance reservation chart, and the hotel directory and rate schedule. (These will be dealt with in chapter 3.)

Information for the Guests

People have come to expect reception personnel to have all sorts of information at their fingertips. They ask questions about car rentals, taxi services, air flights, places of worship, medical or dental services, beauty parlors and hairdressers, places of interest in the area, where to go for entertainment, the best restaurants and night clubs, the availability of theater tickets, and more.

Inquiries regarding the geographical location and places of interest require knowledge of the locality. It is helpful to have a guide book to the area on hand. Details of activities and entertainment in town can be obtained from the entertainment section of the local paper.

Foreign visitors will expect the receptionist to have a knowledge of the country in general and be able to advise on social customs, habits, and language.

Information Regarding Guests

All guests are entitled to a measure of privacy and protection, and any questions about a guest in the establishment should be handled with caution and discretion. One must avoid any publicity that could damage the reputation of the hotel. Any unauthorized person asking for personal information about a guest should be referred to the manager.

COMMUNICATION WITH THE GUEST

Every employee is the personal representative of the establishment and has a public relations job to do. To establish good communication with the guest is part of this job. The guests are paying for service, but it is much nicer if that service is given with a smile by someone who takes a personal interest.

There should always be a willingness to listen and try to understand the guests' anxieties and problems. Always greet the guest warmly and by name, and say something pleasant. Never argue or contradict, and avoid controversial conversations. Do not be too familiar, and remember that "sir" or "madam" are not signs of servility but terms of respect. Immediate attention to a request for information or assistance is a service a guest will appreciate.

Language barriers often create a problem when front desk personnel assist non-English speaking guests. Many hotel chains that cater to a large international clientele have their registration forms and guest service directory printed in several different languages. They employ multilingual staff members, and have an interpreter on call if needed. In the hospitality industry there is a definite advantage to having a basic knowledge of everyday phrases in a number of foreign languages. A greeting or exchange of a few phrases in the visitor's own tongue will certainly help to put the guest at ease, and you may be able to help the guest to better understand the basic layout and policies of the hotel.

It is not hard to please nine out of ten people, so regard the difficult and awkward guest as a challenge that will prove your skill in human relations.

CHAPTER SUMMARY

This chapter discusses the role of the front desk reception associate and the special qualities and social skills desirable for any employee who deals directly with the public. It emphasizes the importance of cleanliness, good grooming, and a pleasant manner that includes tact and diplomacy when dealing with guests or difficult situations.

Important points discussed are:

- Poise and deportment
- Personal appearance and hygiene
- Voice projection and correct speech
- Telephone manner
- Dealing with awkward guests and situations
- Handling inquiries at the front desk
- Good communication with the guests

FOR DISCUSSION

1. Discuss why the front office is considered to be the nerve center of any hotel/motel, whether it be a small or large establishment.
2. Social skills are always important. Discuss why they are considered essential in front desk personnel.
3. You are going for an interview for the position of front desk reception associate in a large hotel. Discuss how you would present yourself for the interview.
4. As a front office manager you have several applicants for a position at the front desk. Discuss the qualities you would look for in each applicant.

KEY TERMS

Charm
Personality
Well groomed
Poise
Deportment
Appearance
Hygiene
Oral communication
Telephone manner
Tact
Diplomacy

CHAPTER QUIZ

1. Write a short paragraph on the desirable qualities of a good reception associate.

2. Write briefly how you, as the person on front desk duty, would deal with a situation where a very agitated guest comes to the desk complaining that she asked for room service an hour ago and is still waiting.

3. "Attention to personal appearance and hygiene are of the utmost importance to a receptionist." Discuss this statement.

4. What are the essentials of a good telephone voice?

5. Explain how you would deal with a very agitated woman on the telephone who wants to speak to the manager because she thinks she has left her valuable watch in the bathroom of her room when she checked out.

6. The vice-president of a local business organization telephones that he wants to hold a dinner party for twenty guests at the hotel. Detail what action you would take.

7. You receive a telephone call from the husband of a guest who is attending a business meeting in the hotel. He asks if you would inform her as soon as possible that her son has met with a serious accident. She is to go straight to the hospital. Describe how you would deal with this situation.

8. Mr. Prentice, a guest, is attending an important business luncheon being held at the hotel; a very hysterical woman who has apparently been drinking, comes to the reception desk, saying she is Mrs. Prentice and demanding that Mr. Prentice be found as she wishes to speak to him. Explain what action you would take to avoid embarrassment to Mr. Prentice and the hotel.

3

THE RECEPTION DESK

No matter what the size of the hotel, motel, inn, or other type of public lodging establishment, the basic work of the front office is the same: selling accommodation, receiving and welcoming guests, maintaining accounting and other records, liaison with other departments within the hotel, and integrating all activities relating to the service and comfort of the guests.

Whether the front office has all the latest computerized equipment or whether it is a small establishment where all records are kept manually, hotel front office operations are based on procedures and principles applicable to all types of establishments, and the following tasks must be dealt with:

1. Reservations
2. Room assignment
3. Guest check-in and registration
4. Guest accounting
5. Credit verification
6. The acceptance of personal and traveler's checks
7. Guest check-out and settlement of accounts
8. Maintaining records
9. Preparing reports and statistics for management
10. Maintaining control procedures

With the exception of certain seasonal resorts, most public lodging establishments, especially the large hotels, operate a twenty-four-hour service, 365 days a year. The front office is usually staffed by a brigade of clerical and reception personnel, working on a rotating schedule to ensure twenty-four-hour coverage. For example, a twenty-four-hour shift might consist of a 7:00 a.m. to 3:00 p.m. shift, a 3:00 p.m. to 11:00 p.m. shift, and an 11:00 p.m. to 7:00 a.m shift. On the night shift, the front desk and switchboard are manned by a small staff and night duty manager.

Most establishments have periods of high and low activity; duty rosters for certain members of staff are planned, therefore, on a split-duty basis. The normal eight-hour shift will be split in some way: four hours on duty, two hours off, four hours on; or four hours in the morning and four hours in the evening; or whatever combination lends itself to the efficient running of the establishment.

The "peak period" for the front office will depend on the type of establishment. At hotels/motels near airports and in major cities visitors arrive and depart at all times, day and night, but daily "peak periods" usually occur in the morning, and again in the afternoon and evening, coinciding with airline departures and arrivals. In resort areas where guest check-in is for a week or more at a time, the busiest time is usually Friday or Saturday. It is the responsibility of the front office manager to plan duty rosters that ensure adequate front desk staffing for "peak periods" so that there are no long lines of guests waiting to check-in or check-out.

In the hospitality industry split duties, weekends, and holidays are normal working periods. People who work in the industry accept and often enjoy this aspect of their work. Career opportunities more than compensate for the unusual hours they are expected to be on duty.

THE RECEPTION AREA

The design, color, and decor of the reception area will depend entirely on the management policies of the individual owners or decisions made at corporate headquarters if the hotel is part of a group. A great deal of market research goes into choosing the theme and decor of a hotel and in particular the reception area. The first impression a guest receives is on arrival at the hotel; the counter and the reception area, therefore, must be pleasing to the eye. The front office is also a functional working area and should be well planned. Work counters should be focused around the major equipment used, and the location should provide for efficient communication and liaison with other sections (fig. 3-1).

It is the responsibility of the desk staff to see that the front desk is kept immaculate at all times. When arriving on duty, personnel should run through the following checklist.

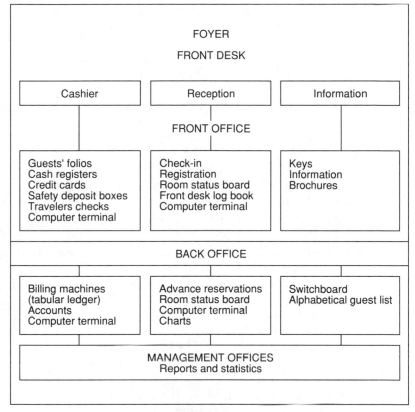

3-1. Simple layout of the reception area.

1. Is the reception desk free from dust and debris? An ample supply of display literature should be kept up-to-date and in its correct place.
2. Have receptacles for cigarette butts and trash been emptied? They should be cleaned throughout the day.
3. Are plant and flower arrangements fresh? Dead leaves should be removed, and artificial arrangements should be kept free of dust.
4. Are the pens in working order? They should be attached to a stand on the counter top.
5. Is the desk calendar visible and is the date correct?
6. The public lodging establishment license issued by the State Department of Business Regulation (see fig. 8-1), the occupational license issued by the city (see fig. 8-2), and the rules and regulations of the establishment should be displayed in a conspicuous place in the reception area.

There are certain basic rules and standards of behavior that managers expect their staff to follow.

1.   Arrive at work on time. It is unfair to other members of staff to arrive late, since the reception desk cannot be left unattended.
2.   If you are unable to report for work your supervisor should be notified immediately so that a replacement can be found.
3.   Desk staff should not eat, drink, or smoke on duty at the reception counter.
4.   Stand when working with a guest. It is unprofessional to address a guest from a sitting position. The front desk associate should always rise when anyone approaches the counter.
5.   Do not lean or lounge on a counter or desk.
6.   Always be polite, helpful, and friendly to guests. If a guest asks a question and you do not know the answer, find out or find someone who does know.
7.   Always be prepared to listen attentively and patiently when a guest talks to you, no matter how boring the subject. Try to develop a technique of being able to detach yourself from a conversation without appearing rude, particularly if there is work to be done or a line of people waiting.
8.   Work quietly; do not shout to other employees.
9.   Never use profanity.
10. Never argue with a guest. In the event of a misunderstanding, call the supervisor or front office manager immediately.
11. Never make an accusation against a guest, or pass any derogatory comments about the character of a guest.
12. The management usually has a ruling that staff members do not socialize with guests on a personal basis. Therefore, staff members should avoid making dates or visiting guests' rooms except in the line of duty.
13. Staff members should not use the bar and lounge facilities of the establishment at which they work, without the approval of the management.
14. Certain areas are set aside for staff members to relax and smoke. These areas should be kept neat and free of litter and dirty ash trays. Cigarette butts should not be thrown on the floor.
15. Drinking and gambling by staff members are not allowed on the premises.
16. Chance-selling, solicitations, and collections are not permitted without the specific approval of the front office manager.

17. Uniforms and name tags must be worn when on duty where applicable.
18. Leave the hotel promptly after your shift is over. Experience has shown that having employees "hanging around" out of uniform creates a bad impression with the guests.
19. Do not give the hotel's address for personal mail.
20. Telephone messages for employees are not acceptable except in the case of emergency or sickness.
21. Wage attachments are a personal embarrassment and a processing expense to the company and should be avoided.
22. It is your responsibility to check the bulletin board daily and read carefully all notices.
23. Do not keep valuables in your locker.
24. Use the special entrance for employees when coming on and going off duty.
25. Parking lots are generally reserved for guests of the establishment. The manager will advise you where employees are allowed to park their vehicles.

THE HOTEL BROCHURE AND TARIFF

Hotel brochures and folders are designed to present the most attractive aspects of the establishment to prospective guests. They are usually very colorful, with photographs that highlight what the hotel has to offer. The hotel tariff is a more low-keyed presentation of the hotel's rates for accommodation and of the services the establishment provides (fig. 3-2).

ROOM RATES

The rates quoted for rooms can vary depending on the type of room offered and the time of the visit. Weekend or holiday rates are often higher than at other times. Resort hotels can also have high, low, or "shoulder" periods depending on their location.

Terminology
Rack rate. The full tariff rate for a room.
Discounted rate. A percentage discount off the rack rate for business travelers, corporations that use the hotel on a regular basis (corporate rate), motoring organizations such as AAA, and other agencies.

Tariff

* * * *   PEACOCK LODGE   * * * *

Jamesville, Florida 34567

(813) 123-4567

ROOM RATES	$
Standard	75
Queen	125
Queen Deluxe	145
King	150
King Leisure	175
Suites	225−375

The above daily rates are on the European Plan subject to bed tax and standard service charge. No meals are included. Rates effective from 1 May 19--.

Reservations must be secured by an advance deposit. It is advisable to secure all golf reservations immediately following confirmation of your reservation.

Green fees for Lodge guests, including cart:

Monte Gordo $65   Bury Hill $45   Regis $25

Tennis court fees: $6 per person per 1 1/2 hours

CHECK-IN TIME:	2:00 p.m.
CHECK-OUT TIME:	11:00 a.m.

No Pets

Rates subject to change without notice.

3-2. Typical tariff of a resort hotel.

Special rates. Negotiated with the management for banquets, conventions, meetings, seminars, and other functions, as well as certain tour groups and organizations.

Low season. The time of year when business is at its quietest. In the northern states, the winter months are slowest except in winter sports areas. In the South, the low season is in summer.

High season. The time of year when business is at its peak and room rates are at their highest.

Shoulder season. The period between high and low seasons.

GUEST SERVICES

A directory of services available to the guest is usually placed in each room. Some of these services have charges, others are free. Typical guest services of a large hotel are:

Airport transportation
Baby-sitting
Baggage handling
Banqueting and catering
Car rental information
Cashier—credit cards, the cashing of personal checks and traveler's checks, foreign currency exchange
Garage parking
Housekeeping for special requests
Information
Room service
Safety deposit boxes
Secretarial
Taxi and limousine
Theater and tour bookings
Florist
Wake-up calls

THE ADVANCE RESERVATION OFFICE

The advance reservation office of the large group and chain hotels, motor hotels, and airlines are linked by computerized central reservation systems. Bimodal reservation systems can link hundreds of hotels in fifty countries, making it possible to make a room reservation almost anywhere in the world via the central system.

Many small and medium hotels, however, still function on a direct, manually operated reservation system. It is essential that the basic principles of charting advance reservations be understood, because even the most sophisticated computer system can fail, and staff may have to revert back to the manual system to keep the flow of business moving.

Personnel working in advance reservations have a great deal of responsibility. It is their job to see that all inquiries for accommodation are dealt with promptly and efficiently. Rooms must be assigned and charted on the reservations and room status charts, so that not only will the guests get the type of accommodation they have requested, but also the establishment will achieve its goal of maximum room occupancy.

A request for a room reservation can be made by telephone, through a central reservation system, telex, or letter, or in person. Whenever a request for accommodation is made the reservations associate must establish:

The name of the guest
Arrival date
Length of stay
Departure date
Type of room required

With this information the clerk is able to check the availability of accommodation and start processing the reservation.

Step-By-Step Procedure on a Manual System

1. When a reservation is confirmed, a room is assigned and penciled in on the advance reservations chart (see figs. 3-9 and 3-10).
2. The reservation form (see fig. 3-3) and copy of the confirmation slip (see fig. 3-4) are filed alphabetically in date-of-arrival order.
3. The guest's name is typed on a strip and inserted in the reception board (see fig. 3-17).
4. A name strip is also typed and inserted in the alphabetical guest list (see fig. 3-27).
5. On arrival the guest completes the registration form (see fig. 3-7) or signs the hotel register (see fig. 3-20). Registration forms are filed in date-of-arrival order.
6. Details of the booking are entered on the room history card (see fig. 3-28).
7. The day prior to arrival the guest's name and the room assigned are entered on the arrivals and departures list (see fig. 3-23).
8. The guest's name and the room assigned are entered on the guest tabular ledger (see chapter 5), and the guest's folio (bill) (fig. 3-8) is started.

If the establishment operates a computerized system, much of the information is fed into the computer and automatically transferred to whatever records the computer is programmed to produce (see chapter 5).

The Reservation Form

Reservation forms are specifically designed to provide all the necessary details and information required to process a booking (fig. 3-3). These include:

1. The date of the receipt of reservation
2. Name and address of the guest
3. Date and time of expected arrival
4. Length of stay
5. Date of departure
6. Advance deposit
7. Method of payment
8. Any special requirements, such as special diets, children's cots, pets, etc.
9. Signature of reservations clerk
10. If the reservation is made by a company or organization, the name and address to whom the account will be sent
11. Room assigned
12. Type of accommodation

Confirmation Slips

If the accommodation is reserved well in advance, it is customary to acknowledge it by sending a confirmation slip (figs. 3-4 and 3-5). The confirmation slip has several copies. The top copy is sent to the guest; other copies are used in the office for the assignment of rooms, charting the reservation, compiling arrivals and departures lists, adding to the alphabetical guest list, and providing information to other departments. The copies are then filed in date-of-arrival order.

Combination Confirmation, Registration, and Guest Folio

Many establishments use specially designed sets of documents to provide them with the information for their records. By use of

```
* * * *   PEACOCK LODGE   * * * *
        Jamesville, Florida 34567
            (813) 123-4567
```

ROOM RESERVATION	DATE	
Name	Date of Arrival	
Address	Time of Arrival	
City State Zip	Date of Departure	
Phone No.	Time of Departure	
Number of Guests	Deposit in Advance	

TYPE OF ACCOMMODATION (Check ✓)		METHOD OF PAYMENT (Check ✓)	
Standard	☐	☐ Cash	
King Leisure	☐	☐ American Express	
King	☐	☐ Mastercard	
Queen Deluxe	☐	☐ Visa	
Queen	☐	☐ Carte Blanche	
Suite	☐	☐ Other	

SPECIAL INSTRUCTIONS:

FOR HOTEL USE ONLY:			
Room allocated		Date	
Key No.		Reservation Clerk	
Rate Code		Reservation by:	
Reservation made by		Phone	☐
Company		Wire	☐
Address		Letter	☐
		In Person	☐
Phone		Acknowledged	☐
Remarks			

3-3. Reservation form.

```
┌─────────────────────────────────────────────────────────────┐
│                                                               │
│          * * * *   PEACOCK LODGE   * * * *                    │
│                                                               │
│              Jamesville, Florida 34567                        │
│                                                               │
│                  (813) 123-4567                               │
│                                                               │
│                  CONFIRMATION                                 │
│                                             No.               │
├───────────────────────────────────────────────────────────────┤
│  Name                              Date:                      │
│                                                               │
│  Address                                                      │
│                                                               │
│  City                  State          Zip                     │
├──────────────┬──────────────────┬─────────┬───────┬──────────┤
│ Arrival Date │ Departure Date    │ Room    │ Rate  │ No. of Persons │
├──────────────┼──────────────────┼─────────┼───────┼──────────┤
│              │                   │         │       │          │
├──────────────┼──────────────────┴─────────┼───────┴──────────┤
│ Arrival Time │        Meal Plan           │ Special Instructions │
├──────────────┼────────────────────────────┼──────────────────┤
│              │                            │                  │
└──────────────┴────────────────────────────┴──────────────────┘
```

Arrival Date	Departure Date	Room	Rate	No. of Persons

Arrival Time	Meal Plan	Special Instructions

METHOD OF PAYMENT (Check ✓)

Cash ☐	Advance Deposit ☐
Check ☐	Date:
Credit Card: American Express ☐	
Mastercard ☐	
Visa ☐	
Carte Blanche ☐	
Other ☐	

Booking Clerk

Please check reverse for important information

3-4. Confirmation slip.

NCR (no carbon required) paper, whatever is typed on the top copy will be recorded on all copies, thus eliminating errors in transferring information. This method is both time and labor saving. The following documents comprise a typical set.

Confirmation slip with copies (fig. 3-6)
Guest registration slip with copies (fig. 3-7)
Guest's folio (bill) with copies (fig. 3-8)

ARRIVAL TIMES

- Room reservations are held until 6:00 p.m., local time, unless later time of arrival is specifically requested.

- Rooms are not normally available before check-out time: 11:00 a.m.

- Check out time is 11:00 a.m. Any request for late check-out should be made to the assistant manager.

- EAP (early as possible) occupancy will be granted if rooms are available upon arrival at the hotel.

CANCELLATIONS/REVISIONS

- Cancellations or revisions of reservation must reach the hotel prior to the time specified on the reservation.

- A minimum of 48 hours notice of cancellation is required for return of deposit.

- Any required deposit specified on the reverse side of the confirmation slip must reach the hotel on the date shown or the reservation will be cancelled.

- The deposit must be made payable to the hotel and sent to the attention of the front office manager.

3-5. Reverse side of confirmation slip.

The Hotel Booking Diary

Some establishments maintain a hotel booking diary, usually a large loose-leaf ledger. A separate page is used for each day. Notes are made on VIP guests, tour groups, meetings, seminars, special events or requests, and the number of guests due to arrive. The diary is used to remind and alert the front office staff of the expected activity of that day.

Room Assignment

The assignment of rooms, which enables an establishment to achieve the maximum occupancy, is a task that requires training, skill, and experience. Many hotels and resorts have agreements with airlines, travel agents, and tour group organizations whereby they reserve a certain number of rooms each night on a guaranteed basis. These

---

* * * *   PEACOCK LODGE   * * * *

Jamesville, Florida 34567

(813) 123-4567

<u>CONFIRMATION</u>

Folio #15150

Surname	Initials	Status	Type of Room	Guaranteed Arrival
				Yes ☐ No ☐

Deposit Requested: Yes ☐   No ☐   Special Instructions:

Code Rate	Arrival Date	Departure Date	No. of Guests	Room Number	Reservation Clerk

The Peacock Lodge is pleased to confirm your reservation.
Your reservation will be held until 6:00 p.m. of your arrival date unless late arrival is guaranteed.
Check-out time is 11:00 a.m. If a late check-out is required please contact the front desk manager.
Check-in time is 2:00 p.m. Guests will be accommodated earlier if rooms are available.
Notification is required 48 hours in advance to return deposit or cancel guaranteed booking.

We look forward to the pleasure of serving you.

FOR HOTEL USE ONLY:

Reservation made by:

Reservation accepted by:

3-6. Combination confirmation slip, registration slip, and guest folio.

rooms are entered on the visual reservations chart automatically as confirmed bookings. Individual reservations are plotted on the chart when confirmed, and walk-in guests as they check-in.

Colored pencil or colored self-sticking tape is used to indicate the type of booking. For example:

Red. Unconfirmed, or not a guaranteed, booking.
Green. Confirmed, a deposit or guarantee received.

```
* * * *  PEACOCK LODGE  * * * *

Jamesville, Florida 34567

(813) 123-4567
```

REGISTRATION FORM

Folio #15150

Surname	Initials	Status	Type of Room	Guaranteed Arrival
				Yes ☐ No ☐

Deposit Requested: Yes ☐   No ☐   Special Instructions:

Code Rate	Arrival Date	Departure Date	No. of Guests	Room Number	Reservation Clerk

GUEST REGISTRATION

METHOD OF PAYMENT

☐ Cash   ☐ American Express

Guest Signature

☐ Check   ☐ Mastercard

Car make. Reg #

☐ Visa   ☐ Carte Blanche

☐ Other

SAFETY DEPOSIT BOXES ARE AVAILABLE
FOR SECURITY OF YOUR VALUABLES.

3-7. Guest registration.

Yellow. Airline or travel agent's guaranteed booking.
Blue. Groups, seminars, meetings, conferences confirmed.
Black. Rooms out of order (OOO).

Unconfirmed reservations usually have a time limit hold period. If by that time (usually 6:00 p.m.) the guest has not arrived or phoned to reconfirm, the room is usually released. A "No Show" means a vacant room unless it is relet. This is a loss of business for the hotel that cannot be regained.

* * * *   PEACOCK LODGE   * * * *

Jamesville, Florida 34567

(813) 123-4567

GUEST FOLIO

15150

Surname	Initials	Status	Type of Room	Guaranteed Arrival
				Yes ☐ No ☐

Deposit Requested: Yes ☐   No ☐   Special Instructions:

Code Rate	Arrival Date	Departure Date	No. of Guests	Room Number	Reservation Clerk

GUEST REGISTRATION

METHOD OF PAYMENT

Guest Signature

Car make. Reg #

☐ Cash   ☐ American Express

☐ Check   ☐ Mastercard

☐ Visa   ☐ Carte Blanche

☐ Other

MEMO #	DATE	REFERENCE	DEBIT	CREDIT	BALANCE	Pick-up Balance

LAST BALANCE IS AMOUNT DUE

Thank You

3-8. Guest folio.

RESERVATION CHARTS

There are many different types of reservation charts in use. Large groups or chain hotel/motels usually have a standard system of charting that enables them to move employees within the group without having to retrain them to the system. Whatever system is used, it is important that the reservations office and front desk have an up-to-the-minute visual picture of room status at all times.

Advance Reservation Power Scan

An advance reservation power scan is a manually operated system that gives an overview of the hotel's room status (fig. 3-9). All rooms of the hotel, floor by floor, are charted on a flat board. A clear white transparency roll with the days of the year at the top revolves from right to left at the touch of a button. Special, colored marking pens that can easily be erased when changes are made are used to block in room assignments. With this type of scan the room reservations for every room for a given day can be brought into view.

The Conventional Chart

This bookings chart (fig. 3-10) can cover three months, with dates clearly marked at the top, and colored pencils used to highlight the weekends. Abbreviations denote the type of room.

Standard	STD
King Leisure	KL
King	K
Queen de luxe	QDLX
Queen	Q
Suite	STE

As bookings are sometimes made months in advance, charts for the year should be prepared. Room rates are marked in pencil to permit erasure in case of change. Entries are made on the chart, also in pencil, as soon as a request for accommodation has been made. When a room reservation has been confirmed it is then marked according to the color code for room assignments—green usually denoting confirmed. Great care must be taken when charting reservations; all entries should be carefully checked to ensure there is no double booking of a room or

JUNE									
	3	4	5	6	7	8	9	10	11
	Sun	Mon	Tues	Wed	Thurs	Fri	Sat	Sun	Mon
Type Room									
STD 401									
STD 402									
STD 403									
STD 404									
STE 405									
KL 406									
K 407									
QDLX 408									
Q 409									
Q 410									

ROOM CHART BOARD

Revolving transparent sheet

Button to revolve scan to left   Button to revolve scan to right

Colored marking pencils used (erasable)

KEY: Red   – Not confirmed
        Green – Confirmed
        Yellow – Airline or travel agents guaranteed
        Blue   – Groups, conferences, seminars
        Black – Rooms 000 (out of order)

3-9. Advance reservation power scan.

Room No.	Type	Rate	1	2	3	4	5	6	7	8	9
		MONTH: JUNE 19 --									
								4TH FLOOR			
401	STD	75.00	WOLF		CANNON						
402	STD	75.00	STEVENS				RYAN				
403	STD	75.00				SMITH					
404	STD	OOO									
405	SUITE	225.00		EWING							
406	KL	175.00	SMITH								
407	K	150.00			JONES						
408	QDLX	145.00			KOJAK						
409	Q	125.00	HORTON		WEISS						

3-10.   The conventional chart.

an uncharted reservation, especially during peak periods when the hotel could be fully booked.

This system has the advantage of presenting a graphic picture showing the bookings and the availability of accommodation at any given period in time.

The Density Chart

The density chart (fig. 3-11) is designed to show at a glance exactly how many and what type of rooms are available. As with the conventional chart, the dates are clearly marked at the top, and the rooms, listed in their different categories, run from top to bottom. A large hotel with several floors will have a density chart for each floor. A large red dot is used to indicate that there are no rooms available in a certain category.

FLOOR 4						MAY 19--					
		1	2	3	4	5	6	7	8	9	10
ROOMS		Sun	Mon	Tues	Wed	Thurs	Fri	Sat	Sun	Mon	Tues
STANDARD	1	X	X	X	X	X					
	2	X	X	X	X	X		X			
	3	X	X	X	X	X	X	X			
	4	X	X				X	X			
	5	X	X				X	X			
	6	X	X				X	X			
	7	X	X			X	X	X			
	8					X	X	X			
	9						X	X			
	10						X	X			
SUITE	1	X	X	X	X	X	X				
KING LEISURE	1	X					X	X			
KING	1					X	X				
QUEEN DELUXE	1	X					X	X			
QUEEN	1	X	X	X	X	X		X			
	2	X	X	X			X	X			
	3					X	X				
	4						X	X			

3-11. The density chart.

Stop–Go Charts

Another type of chart often used is the Stop–Go chart (fig. 3-12). These are prominently displayed to enable the reservations staff to see at a glance whether they can accept a booking for a certain date. There is a chart for each month, a space for each day. Symbols are used to indicate the nonavailability of a certain type of room on a particular day.

From the Stop–Go chart illustrated, the reservations personnel can see that on Friday, 4 May, and Saturday, 5 May, only suites are available. On Friday, 4 June, and Saturday, 5 June, there are no rooms

3-12. Stop–Go chart.

available. On 3, 4, and 5 July there is a convention being held in the hotel, and all rooms are booked. On Friday, 8 July, and Saturday, 9 July, all rooms are booked.

Simultaneous Message Machines

Many hotels use a simultaneous message machine, which is a two-way link between the front desk and the housekeeping department.

When a guest checks-out, the front desk personnel will write a message with the room number informing the housekeeping department that the room is now vacant and needs servicing. When the room has been cleaned the housekeeping staff writes a message on the machine which informs the front desk that the room is ready for letting. This simple device provides instantaneous communication between the two departments and ensures that the room status board has up-to-the-minute information on the availability of rooms.

Electronic Room Status Boards

Many modern hotels have installed electronic room status boards that link the front office not only with housekeeping but with every room. There is a board in the reception office, cashier's office, and housekeeper's office with a button for every room. The system is simple. A green light on the three boards indicates that a room is vacant and has been cleaned and serviced. When a guest checks-in, a room showing a green light is assigned, the button is pressed and the light goes out. When a guest departs, the cashier will press a button and a red light appears, indicating that the room is vacant and ready to be cleaned. The housekeeper then has the room serviced, and when it is ready, presses the button for that room. A green light appears on all boards indicating that the room is again available for letting.

The Whitney System

The Whitney system is a patented system for hotels, whereby the names of guests requesting reservations are typed on stiff paper or cardboard strips and inserted in movable aluminum pockets alphabetically under the date of reservation (figs. 3-13, 3-14). Each evening the rack containing the reservations due to register the following day are removed from the advance reservations rack (fig. 3-15) and placed alongside the room rack (fig. 3-16), becoming the current reservations rack. After serving its purpose it is returned to the advance reservations

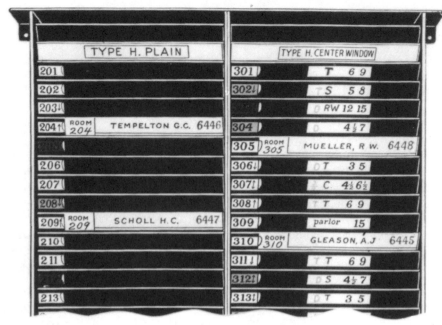

3-13. Room racks (Courtesy of Whitney Duplicating Check Company, New York).

section. These reservation racks replace the hotel's booking diary and are used as arrivals lists for each day in conjunction with the reception board.

The Reception Board

Some smaller establishments use the basic reception board system (fig. 3-17) to give them room status. When a reservation is made a card, typed with the guest's name, date of arrival, date of departure, and room type and rate, is placed in an appropriate room slot. Colored cards or strips denote VIPs, tours, groups, and out-of-order rooms. Since a reception board can only show room status for one day, the conventional, density or power-scan chart is still necessary when selling rooms in advance.

Airline and Travel Agents'
Guaranteed Reservations

Large hotels catering to guests in transit often enter into agreements with certain airlines or tour and travel agents whereby they will

3–14. Combination room and key pocket racks (Courtesy of Whitney Duplicating Company, New York).

3-15. Room rack (Courtesy of Whitney Duplicating Check Company, New York).

3-16. Advance and current reservation rack (Courtesy of Whitney Duplicating Check Company, New York).

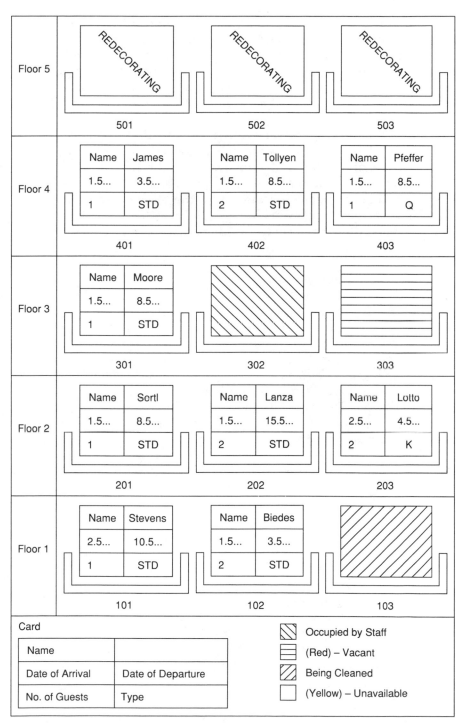

Floor 5	REDECORATING 501	REDECORATING 502	REDECORATING 503

Floor 4

Name	James		Name	Tollyen		Name	Pfeffer
1.5...	3.5...		1.5...	8.5...		1.5...	8.5...
1	STD		2	STD		1	Q

401   402   403

Floor 3

Name	Moore
1.5...	8.5...
1	STD

301   302   303

Floor 2

Name	Sortl		Name	Lanza		Name	Lotto
1.5...	8.5...		1.5...	15.5...		2.5...	4.5...
1	STD		2	STD		2	K

201   202   203

Floor 1

Name	Stevens		Name	Biedes
2.5...	10.5...		1.5...	3.5...
1	STD		2	STD

101   102   103

Card

Name	
Date of Arrival	Date of Departure
No. of Guests	Type

Occupied by Staff

(Red) – Vacant

Being Cleaned

(Yellow) – Unavailable

3-17. The reception board.

hold a number of rooms for them on a guaranteed basis. This means that the airlines or travel agents guarantee to pay for these rooms whether they are used by their clients or not. If they wish to cancel any of the rooms assigned they must do so within the time limit set by the hotel. A typical example of this arrangement is an airport hotel that holds a block of rooms for airline pilots and cabin staff who have stopovers between flights.

Airlines, travel agents, and tour operators offer package tours that include air flight and a number of nights at a certain hotel. In this case, the tour operator makes an agreement with the hotel to reserve the number of rooms required for their clients. The hotel will send the bill for the accommodation used directly to the airline or tour operator. Meals, beverages, and extras are usually paid for separately by the guests unless these are included in the package agreement.

Central Reservation Systems

Most large groups of hotels are linked by a computerized network and operate their own central reservations system. A room-rate availability bank is stored in the computer at a central headquarters. When a client requests a room through the central reservation system, the computer searches its information files and a room-rate availability appears on the screen. If an accommodation is available, the operator confirms the reservation. The hotel, in which the reserved room is located, is signaled with details of the reservation, and the room is deducted from the room availability bank.

If a client makes a reservation by contacting the hotel directly, by telephone or in person, the central computer is signaled by the hotel, and again the sold room is deducted from the room availability bank.

Other centralized reservation systems are not affiliated with any group. They work on a commission basis and hotels, motels, resorts, or other establishments who join the scheme provide details of their location, accommodation, and facilities. The information is fed into the computer bank and guests can be directed to hotels with the type of accommodation, in the location they request.

For the system to function efficiently, the computer bank must have up-to-the-minute information of room-rate availability at all times. Failure to do this could result in over or double bookings, loss of goodwill, and unnecessary charges being levied against the hotel for the service.

Central reservation services have proved invaluable, particularly to overseas and interstate travelers who often have limited knowledge of the areas and accommodations available.

RESERVATION TERMINOLOGY AND RULES

Confirmation. Some hotels send the client a standard form of confirmation to acknowledge a reservation when a deposit has been received.

No confirmation. In large hotels for travelers it is not practical to confirm every reservation in writing. Guests come and go on short notice. Some hotels do telephone a confirmation and will acknowledge receipt of a deposit or special request.

Deposit. Nonrefundable deposits are usually requested from overseas or out-of-state clients booking in advance. The majority of people use credit cards and if they fail to cancel the reservation within the time limit set, or are a "no-show," they will be billed, and forfeit their deposit.

Cancellation. A cancellation means a loss of business unless the room can be relet. Large hotels frequented by travelers are less likely to suffer loss, but resort establishments often request a deposit to confirm the reservation. When a cancellation is received it is imperative that the booking is deleted immediately from all reservation charts and documents throughout the system.

6:00 p.m. release. Most hotels operate on the principle that unless previously notified by the client of a late arrival, the accommodation will be released for reletting if the guest fails to arrive by 6:00 p.m.

No-show. This term is used to indicate the nonarrival of a guest for whom no formal cancellation has been received.

T or P (take or place)—Hotels will sometimes offer T or P bookings to people who are able to accept accommodation at short notice. If there has been a cancellation or no-show, regular clients are offered the accommodation at a reduced rate.

Guaranteed arrival. This type of commitment is usually offered to travel agents, tour operators, and companies who regularly do business with the establishment and can be relied upon to guarantee their commitment. Payment will be made whether the guest arrives or not. This type of guarantee reverses the 6:00 p.m. release procedure and is useful for overseas and interstate travelers whose arrival times are governed by airline, bus, and train schedules.

VIPs or CIPs. Reservations for very important persons (VIPs) or commercially important persons (CIPs) are usually dealt with by senior executives of the hotel or motel. If special arrangements have to be made, a note in the hotel diary will remind the duty manager when VIPs or CIPs are due to arrive.

Special discounts and commissions. Reservations made through travel agents, tour operators, automobile associations, and certain business organizations are usually subject to either special rates or discounts. The front desk should have a note of these rates for guests checking-in.

Hotel discount. Holders of hotel discount cards are clients, businesses, or organizations who use the hotel on a frequent basis. The card entitles them to a percentage discount off the advertised room rate.

Lead time. The time between the booking date and the time of arrival.

Walk-in. A guest who arrives without a reservation.

Stay-on. A guest who extends his/her stay beyond the original date of departure.

Early departure. A guest who checks-out before his/her scheduled date of departure.

Room nights. The number of rooms available multiplied by the number of days covered by the reservations chart. A principle of reservations charts is to show the number of room nights available.

TRAVEL AGENTS, TOUR ORGANIZATIONS, AND GROUP TRAVEL

Today most people rely on travel agents to make their travel arrangements and book their airline tickets and accommodation. Tour operators organize package vacations; other organizations offer group travel. Specialist organizations plan conventions, conferences, seminars, and other types of meetings. These agents work on a commission basis, and special rates and discounts are negotiated with the hotels either through their corporate offices or with the individual hotel. The negotiations depend on several factors:

The amount of business guaranteed by the agents during the high and low season.

The time of year reservations are required.
The time of the week—midweek or weekends.
The number of people in the group.
The type of accommodation required.
The length of time the accommodation is required.
Other facilities required.

Not all establishments will accept package holidays or tour groups. Luxury hotels may only assign 20 percent of their accommodations, whereas other hotels may regard this type of business as their main source of income, assigning 80 percent or more and planning their services around this kind of market.

Tour Booking

When handling tour bookings all details must be thoroughly discussed with the agent before the group's expected arrival. Items such as meal plans, baggage handling, tipping, and methods of payment by the group for any extras should be clarified.

Group Booking Form

The group booking form (fig. 3-18) must be completed by the tour operator. It gives full details of the group's requirements.

Confirmation and Room List

There is usually a cancellation deadline on group reservations, after which the agent will be billed. When finalizing the arrangements and confirming the reservations, the tour operator usually includes the names of all members of the party, rooming requirements, such as family grouping or adjacent rooms, any dietary requests, and so on. Room assignment must be made bearing in mind any special requests. The executive chef must be informed of dietary needs, and housekeeping informed if cots or rollaway beds are needed, and so on.

Group Registration

It is important that each individual member completes a registration form with their own signature, otherwise there could be prob-

				No.				
Group Name:				Tour Operator:				
Group Leader:				Phone No.:				
Number in Group:				Mailing Address:				
Arrival Date: Time:								
Departure Date: Time:								

ACCOMMODATION			MEAL PLAN					
Room	Type	No.	EP	AP	MAP	BP	CP	

SPECIAL REQUIREMENTS:

Subject to terms and conditions on reverse

3-18.   Group booking form.

lems when billing the guests for extras. Groups can register with each member completing an individual registration form upon arrival. With large groups this can cause long lines and chaos at the reception desk. Instead, individual registration forms can be given in advance to the tour operator for completion by the group en route to the hotel. They are handed in to the reception desk upon arrival, with the tour operator's list of the members of the group.

Arrival of Groups

The arrival of large groups of people at the same time will always put pressure on the reception desk, the bell captain's staff, and other departments. If a group arrives in the morning before the housekeeping department has had time to clean and service the rooms, then the group must be made comfortable in one of the public rooms while waiting to gain access to their own rooms. The bell captain's staff will be responsible for unloading the baggage and dispatching it to the rooms as quickly as possible.

Account Charges

Details of what is included in the package rate to be charged to the tour operator will have been finalized before the arrival of the group. It is usual for a group account to be opened, and the hotel will ask that the guests pay individually for extras. A separate guest folio will be opened and extras will be charged to the guest's own room number. Settlement of these accounts is requested before check-out.

A tour operator's voucher will have been sent to the hotel with the confirmation and room list. On check-out the group leader will hand the reception desk a copy of the voucher, signed by the group leader detailing all the charges for which the tour operator will be responsible. The two copies of the voucher and the hotel's group account will be clipped together, checked, and authorized by the front office manager, then forwarded to the tour operator for payment.

Departure of Groups

Like the arrival of a large group, the departure also can be chaotic. It requires organization and planning, as one group often follows another. For the change-over to be smooth, all departments must be working to maximum efficiency. Guests will usually be required to vacate their rooms by 11:00 a.m., noon at the latest. This enables the housekeeping staff to service and clean the rooms for the next arrivals. If the group is not leaving until the afternoon, it is advisable to have a hospitality room available for baggage to be stored and for guests to have access to the restrooms.

The billing office must ensure that all extra charges have been made to the correct accounts, and the bills settled before baggage is removed. Finally all keys must be collected.

Group Bookings, Tours, Conventions, Seminars

An "en bloc" booking means that a number of rooms must be reserved to accommodate a group of people. Before accepting the booking, the reservations chart is studied. If the hotel accepts too many en bloc bookings, it may not be able to accept other kinds of business, such as clients who may return on a regular basis. To avoid this, market research is carried out and management decides what percentage of their business can safely be assigned to en bloc bookings, at special rates.

OVERBOOKING

Under the rules and regulations of the Department of Business Regulations, Division of Hotels and Restaurants, overbooking by a public lodging establishment licensed by the division is prohibited in many states. Through lack of communication or error, occasional overbooking is bound to occur. When it does happen, and an individual or party has a prepaid reservation and is deprived of accommodation, the rules stipulate that the public lodging establishment shall "Make every effort to find other comparable accommodations and, upon demand of the guest, refund all monies deposited for such reservations."

It is the goal of every establishment to achieve maximum room occupancy. A room not sold for a night is a financial loss that cannot be regained. Researchers, therefore, calculate the average percentage of rooms that are left unoccupied. The average number of no-shows, cancellations, and early departures are added up and divided by the number of rooms reserved. This will give the percentage of reserved rooms that are empty on average. For example, on average there are sixteen no-shows, cancellations, and early departures for two hundred reservations. This means that on average, 8 percent of the reservations are not honored.

This figure is noted on the reservations chart. The front office may accept that percentage of reservations above their maximum accommodation. If the unexpected happens, and the hotel is completely full and thus overbooking occurs, there should be a contingency plan agreement with other hotels that have accommodations of the same standard and can accept the overflow. Any additional cost for transporting the guests should be borne by the hotel that accepted the original reservation.

CHECK-IN OF GUESTS

When a guest arrives at the hotel, he/she should have a reservation confirmation number or slip, or a travel agent's or airline's voucher, as evidence of their reservation. These are checked against the hotel's records. In the case of a walk-in, the room status would have to be checked to see if accommodation is available.

Cashing of Checks

As it can take ten days or more for an out-of-state check to clear, some hotels set limits on the check amount they will cash. The guest is always required to give proper identification—e.g., a credit card or driver's license.

Credit Card Approval

Credit cards are now considered a more acceptable method for settling accounts, since the credit card companies guarantee settlement of the bill up to the credit limit extended to their clients (see chapter 5). If a guest has indicated that he or she intends to settle by credit card, upon check-in the credit card is requested and an imprint of the card is taken and held for signature when the guest wishes to settle the account.

Many hotels now have a credit card microphone machine, which is linked to a central computer serving the major credit card companies (see chapter 5). By putting the card into the machine an approval or disapproval code number will be shown on the visual digital screen. If there is no machine the hotel can telephone the credit card bank of the company and request the approved code as to the credit-worthiness of the card holder. If the credit approval is declined the management must contact the guest immediately. Guests who are not holders of a credit card are usually asked to pay in advance for their accommodation, and all other incidentals in bars and restaurants are offered on a cash basis.

Identity Booklets

It is now common practice in the large hotels to issue guests upon arrival identity booklets in attractively designed folders (fig. 3-19). The booklets are also designed to advertise and highlight the features and facilities of the hotel, including a list of direct-dialing telephone numbers for all services.

The name of the guest, room number, and key code number which, for security reasons, are different from the actual room number,

Front   Back

```
                                    TELEPHONE DIRECTORY

                                         Guest Services
                                     Assistance Information
                                           ext. 1250

         PEACOCK                                              ext.
         LODGE                       Assistant Manager        1297
                                     Bell Captain             1365
                                     Front Office             1271
                                     Housekeeping             1285
                                     Room Service             1291
FOLD                                 Wake-Up Service             0      FOLD
                                     Pavilion Restaurant      1273
                                     Tartan Bar               1274
                                     Jingles Night Club       1276
                                     Room Reservations        1180
                                     Tours and Transportation 1257
Tel: (813) 123-4567                  Theater Tickets          1257
```

Inside

* * * * WELCOME TO THE PEACOCK LODGE * * * *

If you presented a credit card upon check-in simply fill out the information
below and leave this card at the front desk on the day of your departure,
without standing in line.

Your account will be processed through your cedit card and if you desire
we will send you an itemized statement immediately upon your departure.

- -

EXPRESS CHECK OUT

Signature

I plan to leave at . . . . on . . . .
                        time   date

　　　I will not require an itemized statement ☐
　　　Please send a copy of my hotel account to:

NAME. . . . .   ZIP . . . .
ADDRESS . . . .
GUEST NAME . . . .

Room No.   Key Code No.

PLEASE LEAVE THIS CARD AT THE FRONT DESK ON THE
DAY OF DEPARTURE

3-19.   Identity booklets.

are printed inside. If guests settle their account by credit card they can take advantage of an express check-out service if one exists.

Special color-coded booklets are used for VIP guests or regular clients of the hotel and carry added privileges such as express check-in and check-out, special rates, welcome cocktails, daily newspapers, and other complimentary features.

Receiving and Registering Guests

The law requires that guests must register with the hotel (see chapter 8). Some small hotels/motels still maintain a hotel register (fig. 3-20), but most hotels now use printed registration forms (fig. 3-7). They have many advantages.

- They are neat, legible, easily handled, and can be filed in chronological order.
- The information on them is confidential; it ensures that only the guest and the hotel front office see that information.

HOTEL REGISTER					
Sheet #			Date:		
Name	Address	Room No.	Time of Arrival	Time of Departure	Car Make and Reg. No.

3-20. The hotel register in book form.

- In the case of a group booking or a line at the reception desk, several guests can complete their registration forms at the same time.
- International hotels can produce the registration forms in several languages, which is a great asset to foreign visitors.
- The registration forms can easily be checked against the original reservation.

When receiving guests at a hotel, the same procedure is followed.

1. On arrival the guests are assisted with their baggage by the baggage handler, who will escort them to the reception counter.
2. The reception associate welcomes the guest with a smile and greeting, hands the pen to them, asking if they will please complete the registration form (fig. 3-7).
3. The registration form is checked to ensure it has been correctly completed.
4. The identity booklet or key card, together with any messages or letters that may be waiting for the guest, are handed to them. In the case of a group checking in, room keys, identity booklets, and information sheets are put in individual envelopes for distribution by the group leader.
5. The reception staff or baggage handler should inform guests of the location of restaurants, lounges, other public rooms and facilities, and emergency exits.
6. The baggage handler will escort the guests to their rooms, offering to carry any hand baggage and walking a few steps ahead to open any doors.
7. The escort should precede the guests into the room, make a quick check to see that the room is in order, and then hand the key to the guest, inquiring if he can be of any further help.
8. In the front office the guests' names are checked off the arrivals and departures list and their folio (bill) started.

VALUABLES FOR SAFEKEEPING

The hotel has no liability for guests' property and is not obliged to accept valuables such as money, jewelry, and furs for safekeeping. However, most hotels do accept a limited liability for valuables left for safekeeping; guests should be asked to give the estimated value of these valuables.

A receipt is given which states that the hotel will not be liable for any loss exceeding a certain amount, unless the loss was the proximate result of fault or negligence of the operator (see chapter 8). To overcome the problem of room security, many hotels are installing small safes right in the room which can be rented at a nominal charge.

Safety Deposit Boxes

Many hotels have safety deposit boxes, similar to those in a bank, for use by their guests. The type and model vary, but usually the guest is given one key to the box for which a signature is required, and the particulars are recorded in a key receipt book. The cashier holds the other key. The safety deposit box can only be opened if both locks are operated at the same time.

LETTER AND KEY RACKS

The letter and key racks (fig. 3-21) are usually located behind the front desk. They consist of a number of pigeonholes large enough to hold regular size mail, with a key hook above. Each pigeonhole in the rack is clearly numbered by floor and by room. In it, incoming mail, small packages, and any messages for guests are left. Keys not in use are hung on the appropriate hooks.

Keys

Master keys that open all doors are held by a few senior members of staff, such as managers, housekeeper, and bell captain. There are at least two sets of keys for every room. The first set is handed to the guest and the second is kept on a duplicate key board, under strict supervision of the front office staff.

Guests should be encouraged to hand in the keys if they leave the hotel, and collect them again upon their return. Care must be taken that the keys are always placed on the correct hook and supervised. For security reasons a regular check must be made on the key rack in case any keys go astray.

Electronic Key System

To overcome the problem of lost keys and to combat the security risk of unauthorized persons getting hold of keys, many hotels are

3-21. Letter and key racks (Courtesy of Whitney Duplicating Check Company, New York).

installing keyless locks on their rooms. This is an electronic system whereby the guest is given a plastic key card (fig. 3-22). A computerized console in the front office programs the key card with a new code every time a new guest uses a room. In essence, it is like changing the locks for every guest.

There is no room number on the key card, and only the correct code will open the door. If a guest loses a key card, a new key card with a new code is issued. The old key card is invalidated on the computer's console, and only the new card code will open the door to the room.

THE ARRIVALS AND DEPARTURES LIST

All departments must be notified of impending arrivals and departures. The housekeeping department must make sure that all

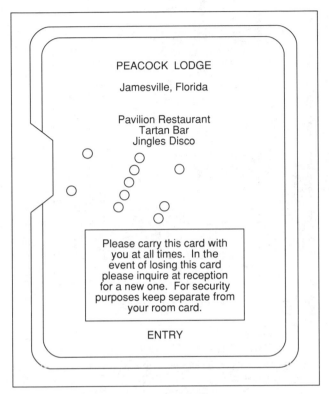

3-22.   Electronic key.

rooms are prepared for new arrivals, so when a room is vacated the maids change the linen and towels and clean the room for the next guest. The restaurant manager and executive chef need to know the estimated number of guests in the hotel and any special dietary needs, in order to plan their menus and prepare for service. The bar managers need to ensure that the bars are adequately staffed and stocked. The bell captain needs to organize his staff schedules for dealing with baggage. Arrivals and departure lists (fig. 3-23), therefore, are prepared by the front office daily, and copies circulated to all departments.

Notification Memos

Because the arrivals list is made up from advance reservations, it will not show the walk-in guests or the guests who change their rooms. Since room status information must be up-to-the-minute, notification

Date: Sheet #

ARRIVALS

Room	Type	No. of Guests	Name	No. of Nights	Time of Arrival	Notes
301	STD	2 + 1 Child	Moore	7	11:30 A	Child's Cot
209	Q	Change of Rm.	Yew	4		*
102	Q	3	Reeve	2	12:00 N	
401	STD	1	Brown	2	1:00 P	
107	Q	3	Jones	5	3:00 P	
5	2 STD 3 Q	9 + 1 child				

DEPARTURES

Room	Type	No. of Guests	Name	Time of Departure	Notes
103	STD	Change of Rm.	Yew		*
304	STD	3	Smith	9:00 A	
401	STD	4	Wilson	11:00 A	
3	3 STD				

*Indicates internal transfer from one room to another.

3-23. The arrivals and departures list.

memos, such as the arrivals memo in figure 3-24, are circulated to all departments updating room status. If the hotel has a computer terminal in each department then the information is fed into the computer.

Walk-in Guests

Walk-in guests are those who arrive without a reservation. If the guest has no luggage, payment by cash in advance is usually requested. If the guest has identification and credit cards, no deposit is requested. Tact should always be used when asking for payment in advance, but the hotel must be protected against fraud so this is a necessary precaution (fig. 3-24).

Change of Room

If a guest wishes to change rooms and the arrival has already been entered on the arrivals and departures list, the change of room must be treated as a departure from one room and an arrival in another room. Because the change of room will have no effect on the number of guests staying in the hotel, no entry is made in the column showing the number of guests. If the arrivals and departures list has already been circulated, a change-of-room notification memo must be sent to all departments informing them of the room change (fig. 3-25).

ARRIVALS MEMO			No. 135	Distribution to:	
Date:	May 1, 19--	Time:		Manager	✓
				Cashier	✓
Name:	JAMES	Room No.	205	Billing Office	✓
No. of guests:	3	Type:	Q	Housekeeper	✓
No. of nights:	2	Rate:	$75	Bell Captain	✓
				Switchboard	✓
Notes:	Walk-in	Meal Plan:	MAP	Restaurant Manager	✓
				Bars Manager	✓
Signature:				Room Service	✓
				Reservations	✓

3-24. Arrivals memo.

ROOM-CHANGE MEMO			No. 272	Distribution to:	
Date:	May 1, 19--	Time:		Manager	✓
				Cashier	✓
Name:	YEW	From Room No. 103		Billing Office	✓
No. of guests:	3	To Room No. 209		Housekeeper	✓
No. of nights:	4	Rate:	$75	Bell Captain	✓
				Switchboard	✓
Notes:	STD for Q	Meal Plan:	MAP	Restaurant Manager	✓
				Bars Manager	✓
Signature:				Room Service	✓
				Reservations	✓

3-25. Room-change memo.

Procedures for Departures

As with arrivals, certain basic procedures are followed at a guest's departure.

1. The billing office will check that all charges and payments have been posted to the guest's account and have it ready to present to the guest at check-out.
2. The cashier will ensure that any valuables left in the hotel's safe or in a safety deposit box are handed to the guest, and that the guest sign a receipt and return the safety deposit box key.
3. The bell captain will have his staff ready to handle baggage. Some hotels give a baggage clearance slip when the account is settled, and the bell captain will clear baggage on receipt of the slip. He will then check departing guests off his departures list.
4. When the room has been checked and cleared, the head housekeeper will check outgoing guests off her departures list.
5. Once the account is settled, keys handed in, and baggage cleared, the guest departs with a warm invitation to return.

The front office will then amend their records as follows:

1. The guest's name is removed from the reception board (see fig. 3-17).
2. The name strip is removed from the guest's alphabetical list (see fig. 3-27).

3. Date of departure is noted on the room history card.
4. If the hotel maintains a guest history card (see fig. 3-29), details and any comments on the guest's stay are entered.
5. If a mail-forwarding form has been completed it is filed alphabetically (see fig. 6-1).

Daily Summary Report

Daily summary reports are prepared for management and other heads of departments (fig. 3-26). They are for information, statistical reports, and cross-checking purposes.

BASIC FRONT OFFICE DUTIES IN A SMALL OR MEDIUM-SIZE HOTEL

A large percentage of establishments in the hotel industry are either small or medium-size, individually owned, and do not warrant the installation of expensive computerized systems. They can be run quite efficiently by a well-trained staff, operating a partially manual system.

The front office is centralized and the duties of the personnel are many and varied. They receive and register guests, deal with advance reservations, handle inquiries, and maintain records. The following tasks should also be part of a daily routine checklist.

DAILY SUMMARY REPORT	Date: June 30, 19--		Distribution to:	
No. of Rooms	Details	No. of Guests	Manager	✓
			Cashier	✓
133	Guests last night	266	Billing Office	✓
42	Departures	72	Housekeeper	✓
91	Sub Total	194	Bell Captain	✓
24	Arrivals	30	Restaurant Manager	✓
5	Walk-Ins	8	Bars Manager	✓
120	Guests tonight	232	Reservations	✓
Signature:				

3-26. Daily summary report.

Morning Duties

- Check the night shift incident log book for any matters that need to be dealt with.
- Sort mail, deal with any that requires attention, and distribute to the appropriate department.
- Check cash floats and prepare them for collection by department managers. These are the set sums of money for cash registers in the restaurants and lounge bars that provide change at the start of the day's business.
- If there is no night audit staff, enter the late night arrivals on the previous day's guest tabular ledger, and start a guest's folio. Balance and close the tabular ledger (see chapter 5), and complete the daily summary report.
- Enter any room service, telephone calls, newspapers, and other guest's charge slips or paid-outs on the guest ledger and the guest's folio.
- Prepare all bills for departing guests, and check that all charges have been posted to the guest folio.
- Type and photocopy menu inserts if necessary.
- Write up and balance cash books (see chapter 5).
- Prepare cash, credit card sales slips, and checks for depositing in the bank.
- During the morning, check to be sure that all departing guests have settled their accounts by check-out time.
- Compute a mid-day balance on the guest tabular ledger (see chapter 5).
- Post any charge slips for lunch, lounge drinks, room and valet service, and so on to the guest ledger and guest folios.
- Update the incident log book. Most hotels keep an incident/log book to record any unusual happenings during the course of the shift. It is not necessary to write a long report. A typical entry includes the date, time, and essential details. It is signed by the person making the entry. For example:

> July 1 Time 8:00 a.m.—Mrs. Jones, Room 112, complained of too much noise coming from Room 110, asked to change room. Transferred to room 120. All departments notified. (signature)
> Time 12:00 noon—Mrs. Brown, Room 108, wishes to extend her stay for two nights, July 8 and 9. Please inform her on room availability for those dates. (signature)

- Before the change in shift, double check to ensure that all work has been processed as far as possible, and note any messages or matters to be dealt with by the next shift.

Evening Duties

- Check incident log book for unfinished business.
- Recheck cash floats to ensure that cashiers have enough change for the evening business.
- Deal with new arrivals and walk-ins, and start guest folios.
- Deal with any correspondence left over from the early shift.
- Post outstanding charge slips to guest ledger and guest folios.
- Check and post accounts payable to accounts payable ledger (see chapter 5).
- Type arrivals and departures list for the next day; photocopy and distribute to all departments.
- If machine accounting is used, take the roll out of the machine, change the date, and check all totals to make sure they are at zero.
- Check the housekeeper's room vacancy report and note room availability (see fig. 7-3).
- Prepare night duty manager's report, with details of rooms available for letting, details of any late arrivals, and the rooms assigned to them.
- Prepare daily reports of the day's business for management.
- Prepare next day's guest ledger (if manual).
- Check all cash received from restaurants, bars, and lounges, and put in safe.
- Check all cash floats, place in safe, lock all cupboards.
- Make entries in log, and leave any messages for night and morning shifts.

All of these duties are discussed in detail in later chapters.

RECORDS

Alphabetical Guest List

It would be impossible for the staff to memorize all the guests' names, particularly in a large hotel. To help facilitate the delivery of messages and distribution of mail, an alphabetical guest list is maintained, usually on a revolving stand located in an area easily accessible to all personnel in the front office (fig. 3-27). These stands can hold

3-27.   Alphabetical guest list (Courtesy of Roneo Ltd.).

several hundred strips, on which are typed the guest's surname, initial, and room number. Color coding indicates the type of room—suite, king, queen, or standard, for example. The strips are inserted in strict alphabetical order.

Writing of Names

A standard, consistent method of writing names should be adopted. In many cases, the following style is used: surname first, written or typed in block capitals, followed by the title of the guest, then the initials. "Mc" and "Mac" are all treated as Mac; the next letter after "C" determines the position.

> BARTON   Mr./Mrs. R. J. & B. L.
> CARSON   Mrs./Ms. P. & J. J.
> HERNANDEZ   Capt./Mrs. R. S. & V.
> MCALLISTER   Sir Robert/Lady Diane
> MACDONALD   Senator/Mrs. K. & E.
> SAINT-JAMES   Dr./Mrs. S. & L.
> ST-CLAIRE   Governor/Mrs. R. & A.
> SATORI   Rev./Mrs. L. & W.
> VELLOCI   Mr./Master T. & T. L.

Room History Record

Most hotels keep a room history card showing when and by whom the room was occupied (fig. 3-28). The cards are filed in room-number order and kept up to date. Much use is made of these cards. For

ROOM-HISTORY CARD			
Room Number Rate			Type
Name	Arrival	Departure	Remarks

3-28. Room-history card.

example, if property has been lost or found in a room, the room history card will show who the occupant was on a given date.

Room Inventory Cards

Room inventory cards are sometimes back-to-back with the room history card. The inventory card states the type of room and furnishings. Any maintenance, repairs, or renewals are noted on the card. These cards are used by housekeeping and maintenance staffs, whose responsibility it is to see that the rooms conform to required standards and no contents go astray.

Guest History Card

For advertising, promotion, and market research, as well as for record purposes, some hotels maintain guest history cards (fig. 3-29). They show the name and address of the guest, dates of visit to the hotel, type of room occupied, room rate, credit rating, patronage, special likes and dislikes. These cards are filed alphabetically and provide useful information as to the type of service to offer the guest and how to cater to his/her preferences. They are useful in maintaining good public relations.

		GUEST HISTORY CARD				
NAME:				**CAR MAKE:**		
ADDRESS:				**REG. NO.:**		
Room #	Date of Arrival	Date of Departure	Room Rate	Total Bill	Paid by	Remarks
206	3/29/19−−	4/1/19−−	$58.00	$136.00	V	Refer to manager Habitually drunk, causing offense to other guests
■■■ (A black sticker to indicate guest on black list)						

3-29.   Guest-history card.

Undesirable Guests

Some visitors may have proved to be undesirable or objectionable, or perhaps left without paying their bill. It is essential to keep a record of these guests for future reference. Because the guest history card is filed alphabetically, colored stickers can be used. A black one might indicate that in the future this person would be considered an undesirable guest.

Reference Books

An efficiently organized front office should always have an up-to-date library of reference books and information literature in order to be able to answer innumerable and varied questions. Such a library might include some of the following.

Dictionary
Telephone directories—both white and yellow pages
Timetables for local public transportation—bus, subway, train

Telephone numbers of airlines and taxi and limousine ser-
vices
Maps of the area
Auto club travel guidebooks for the area
Local newspapers
Entertainment guides for the area
Lists of local medical services, from clinics and hospitals,
to doctors, dentists, ophthalmic surgeons, and optom-
etrists
Lists of local churches and their denomination
Brochures and literature on local places of interest
Calendar of local events
Area code maps and listings
International long distance telephone codes and city codes
List of state and local government offices

COMMUNICATIONS

Communication systems are now becoming so sophisticated that
it is only a matter of time before people will only have to press a button
on the telephone to see the person to whom they are talking. Already
Picturephone Meeting Services are in wide use. These enable business
executives to meet face-to-face with their key managers, even with
continents between them. For a reasonable charge, in-room personal
computers are now being made available by some of the major hotel
groups.

Private Branch Exchange (PBX)

The telephone service in most establishments involves the use of a
PBX switchboard with one or more lines, and extensions in the various
offices and departments (fig. 3-30). In hotels/motels, there are usually
telephones in all rooms. Switchboard operators should put through calls
with minimum delay and maximum courtesy.

Private Automatic Branch Exchange (PABX)

The PABX system combines exchange services with automatic
communications facilities. Each telephone has its own dial; from it,
other extensions within the hotel, as well as outside calls, can be dialed.

3-30.   A private branch exchange (PBX) system (Courtesy of AT&T).

Emergency Numbers

Most communication systems list the following numbers: emergency numbers for fire, police, highway patrol, sheriff, and ambulance service; FBI and U.S. Secret Service. These are found at the front of the telephone directory. Front desk personnel should become familiar with these numbers to avoid delay in the case of an emergency.

Area Code Maps

With travelers moving all over the country, an area code map and area code listings should be on hand to avoid delay in providing information for a guest wanting to make a long distance call.

International Long Distance Calls

The front desk must be able to assist visitors in placing international telephone calls. A list of country and city codes can usually be found in the front of the telephone directory.

Other Types of Calls

The front desk must always be willing to assist guests with the terminology and services provided by U.S. telecommunications systems such as:

Station-to-station. The caller will talk to anyone who answers.

Person-to-person. The caller only wishes to speak with a particular person.

Collect call. The person you wish to talk to must agree to accept the charge.

Calling-card service. Callers who have a calling card provided by their telephone company may place a call, quoting the calling card number and having it charged to their own telephone account.

800 toll-free service. Station-to-station and long distance calls may be made to businesses that have an 800 listing free of charge to the caller. Most central reservation services, for example, have an 800 listing.

Time and charges. Callers may request the operator to give them the time and cost of their call.

Conference calls. It is possible to talk to several people in different places at the same time by arranging a conference call through the operator. Most telephone companies have special conference-call operators to handle this service.

Busy-signal verification. If a caller repeatedly gets a busy signal, he/she may request the operator to verify that the line is in working order.

Emergency interrupt line. If there is an emergency situation and the line is busy, you may ask the operator to interrupt the conversation and request that the line be cleared so that your call may be completed.

Advance Communication Systems

Modern microprocessors and computer technology have made such rapid advances that telecommunications and internal communications systems are now compact, lightweight units, without plugs, switches, or buttons. Small keyboards with touch-sensitive depressions, some with visual display units (VDUs) that can show at a glance the status of all calls being handled, can guide the operator through every step. Training is reduced to a minimum.

Modern communication systems have as many exchange lines and extensions as a subscriber may need. The system can be tailored to meet the requirements of any business. There are computer property-management systems for hotels, resorts, and managements companies coming on the market all the time. Systems, such as in-room video check-out service, whereby guests can review their bills and authorize check-out by pressing a button on their television set, are now available in many locations. Guests can either pick up a printed copy at the express desk in the hotel lobby or have it mailed to them within twenty-four hours.

Other videotech services will link the guest in his room to an enormous range of computer-held information that can be brought to the television screen at the touch of a button.

Special Communication Features for Hotels

> **Electronic room status boards.** The status of every room can be displayed. The front office can tell at a glance whether a room is occupied, waiting to be serviced, or ready for the next guest.
>
> **Wake-up calls.** Guests can program their own wake-up calls on the telephone.
>
> **Message waiting.** The switchboard can be programed to call a guest's room automatically at regular intervals until a reply is received.
>
> **Call metering.** Guests can make their own private calls and the metered units will be recorded automatically against their room number. The station message detail recording (SMDR) system will print out details of calls made.
>
> **Room monitors.** The front office can monitor a room in which a child has been left.
>
> **Priority calling.** Preferential telephone service can be given to VIPs.
>
> **Room service.** Direct inward dialing (DID) enables the guest to bypass the receptionist, and call the hotel services direct.
>
> **Do not disturb.** Calls are kept from ringing in the room.
>
> **Outgoing call restriction.** Expensive unofficial calls are kept to a minimum. The system can be instructed to restrict out-

going calls, such as long distance or international direct dialing (IDD) from certain telephones.

Telex and Teleprinter

A teleprinter is a machine with a typewriter keyboard on which messages can be reproduced on another teleprinter at the end of the wire. Modern technology is now so advanced and sophisticated that the latest teleprinters have enormous power and flexibility. Some features of the modern teleprinter include the following:

- Alphanumerical keys, as on a conventional typewriter.
- Integrated visual display units (VDUs).
- Telex messages can be typed directly into the teleprinter's memory and automatically transmitted at a preset time.
- Messages can be received and transmitted automatically while the operator is preparing another message on the screen.
- Incoming messages can be stored in the teleprinter's memory until the printer is free or, by pressing a button, the incoming message can be given priority.
- The same message can be transmitted to several different destinations.
- The contents of any message stored in the teleprinter's memory can be recalled and displayed on the visual display unit.
- Word-processing features allow for fast and efficient editing of messages.

Facsimile Communication

FAX machines can transmit facsimiles of typed or handwritten documents, graphic designs, and photographs over the telephone to other FAX machine numbers. The basic process is as follows:

- The FAX machine scans a document converting its dark marks to digital pulses that are changed to voice tones that are conveyed over telephone lines. At the receiving end the digital pulses are reconverted and print the black marks onto paper.
- The document to be transmitted feeds automatically into the FAX machine. The FAX telephone number to which the document

is being sent is dialed. At the "beep" signal the "start" button is pressed and the telephone receiver is replaced.

- The FAX machine at the receiving end of the transmission automatically prints out a facsimile of the document. A readout sheet on the sending FAX machine acknowledges receipt.
- Desktop FAX machines are compact and lightweight and can be hooked up to a computer system. Portable machines can be operated from a car.

CHAPTER SUMMARY

This chapter deals with the basic principles and practices of front office reception procedures, whether in a small, medium, or large establishment. Not all establishments are fully computerized; many still work on partial manual systems. Whatever system is used, front office personnel must understand the basic procedures to be followed when dealing with reservations, room assignment, arrivals and departures of guests, credit verification, account settlement, recordkeeping in accordance with state, federal, and internal revenue service regulations, preparing reports and statistics, and maintaining control systems.

If an establishment is fully computerized, the front office personnel must comprehend the nature of the information that is fed into the system and the data and records that the system produces.

Important points and topics discussed are:

- Room rates
- Guest services
- Advance reservations
- Operating a manual system
- Reservation charts
- The Whitney system
- Guaranteed reservations
- Central reservation systems
- Travel agents, tour organizations, and group travel
- Overbooking
- Checking-in guests
- Handling credit cards and cashing checks
- Receiving and registering guests
- Valuables for safe-keeping
- Communicating with other departments of the hotel

- Front office duties in a small or medium establishment with a partially manual system
- Recordkeeping
- Communication systems

FOR DISCUSSION

1. Discuss the first impressions you get when you arrive as a guest at a hotel.
2. The management of an establishment usually sets rules and standards of behavior for the staff to follow. Discuss the reasons why management feels it necessary to set such rules and standards.
3. Compare the types of services offered by luxurious, average, and small establishments, and discuss the types of services you would consider to be essential and nonessential.
4. Discuss the advantages and disadvantages of using a central reservation system.
5. Discuss the effects of computer system failure in the front office of a hotel. What back-up system would you recommend in the advance reservations office so that the flow of business was not interrupted and advance reservations could be charted?
6. Discuss the different kinds of problems that arise at the front desk when a very large tour group arrives.
7. Discuss the problems that can arise at the front desk through over or double booking. How would you solve them?
8. Discuss the basic duties of a front desk reception associate working in a small hotel, operating with a partially manual system.

KEY TERMS

High and low activity
Low season
High season
Shoulder season
Rack rate
Discounted rate
Special rate

Central reservation system
Advance reservation power scan
Conventional reservation chart
Density chart
Stop–Go chart
The Whitney system
Guaranteed reservation
Confirmation
Deposit
Cancellations
6:00 p.m. release
No-show
T or P
Special discounts
Commission
Lead time
Walk-in
Early departure
Hotel discount
VIP and CIP
Overbooking
Doublebooking

CHAPTER QUIZ

1. Define the following terms:
    a. Rack rate
    b. Discounted rate
    c. Shoulder period
    d. VIP and CIP
    e. T or P
    f. Walk-in
    g. No-show
    h. 6:00 p.m. release
    i. Guaranteed arrival
    j. Hotel discount card

2. Define the use and purpose of the following, using simple diagrams to illustrate your answers where necessary.
    a. The conventional reservations chart

    b. A reception board
    c. The power-scan reservations chart
    d. The arrivals and departures list
    e. The alphabetical guest list

3. How would a hotel check the credit-worthiness of a guest?

4. The hotel receives a call from Mr. and Mrs. K. Horton who wish to reserve a king-size room from 7–14 June. Your hotel uses a manual system. Explain how you would process the reservation and stay, from the date of the request to final departure of the guests.

5. Explain briefly how:
    a. the Whitney reservations system operates
    b. an electronic status board operates
    c. an electronic key system operates, and describe its advantages

6. The Silver Star tour organization wishes to reserve accommodation for a group of twenty people on a package tour. Detail the step-by-step procedure for handling the booking from the time the inquiry is made to the final departure of the group.

7. Explain briefly how a central reservations system operates.

8. A guest wishes to change rooms. What action would you take to ensure that all records are amended and all departments notified?

9. A group of five guests is coming in on a late plane and will not arrive until 9:00 p.m. What action should be taken and what instructions will you leave for the evening shift?

10. You are the front office manager of a medium-size hotel instructing a new trainee at the reception desk. Explain briefly how you would describe the tasks that have to be carried out:
    a. on the morning shift, from 7:00 a.m.–3:00 p.m.
    b. on the evening shift, from 3:00 p.m.–11:00 p.m.

11. Explain the following telecommunications terms:
     a. station-to-station call
     b. person-to-person call
     c. collect call
     d. conference call
     e. emergency interrupt
     f. calling-card service

12. Explain the basic difference between the teleprinter and FAX, and the advantages of both.

13. List the reference books and literature that are needed to answer possible inquiries from guests.

4

SELLING AND
MARKETING

Successful selling not only maximizes the profitability of the establishment, but also promotes good customer relations. Satisfied guests become word-of-mouth salesmen, promoting the hotel and its services.

FRONT OFFICE RECEPTION
AS A SALES DEPARTMENT

In order to sell accommodation successfully, reception desk personnel must learn how to use their eyes, ears, and intelligence to assess clients and their needs. All guests will differ emotionally, physically, and temperamentally, and will have a wide variety of likes and dislikes, tastes and income levels. In the hospitality business, employees come into contact not only with people from all over this country, but also visitors from abroad. It is part of the job to be able to adapt and handle people from all walks of life.

As the management set maximum occupancy and profitability as their goal, the front office staff must be trained to assign rooms on the reservations charts so that one reservation follows another and there are no unnecessary gaps left. Charting reservations successfully takes training, skill, practice, and experience.

Guidelines to Selling Accommodation

1. Whenever possible, let rooms floor-by-floor, from the ground up, grouped together. This helps the housekeeping department organize the maid service more efficiently.
2. The management will obviously expect their staff to sell the higher priced accommodation whenever possible, but remember that a room empty for a night is a sale lost forever.
3. Select and offer rooms within the price range appropriate to the guest.
4. Always tactfully ascertain whether a couple prefers a double bed or two beds.
5. Offer families adjoining or adjacent rooms.
6. Bear in mind when assigning rooms that elderly, handicapped, or disabled people will not want stairs to climb or long walks to elevators, restaurants, or lounges.
7. Before offering accommodation, ask the guests if they have any preferences: nonsmoking, room with a view, back room away from the noise of the highway, a particular floor, and so on.
8. If all standard rooms are sold and the hotel is not full, the management may have a policy of offering the higher priced rooms at a reduced rate rather than not sell at all. This may depend on the time of day, such as late evening. In this situation the front desk will have the reduced rates on hand and may offer them to walk-in guests.

In any organization, people are either the strongest or weakest link, and all operations within that business will depend on their ability to listen, think, remember, communicate, and act. Their performance will invariably have a profound effect on the selling of the product—which in the hotel industry is accommodation, hospitality, food, and drink.

There is no substitute for knowledge. The front office staff of an establishment must have not only all the social skills mentioned in chapter 2, but also a complete knowledge of the product they are selling—the hotel—if they are going to sell it effectively.

Front office personnel must be thoroughly familiar with the following:

* All information in the hotel's brochures and folders.

- Details of all tariff charges including charges for children, pets, and the use of extras such as tennis courts and golf courses.
- Any special rates and discounts that are offered.
- All general facts and figures pertaining to the establishment, for example, its size, room categories, their furnishings and facilities. Any special information regarding banqueting or conference facilities, swimming pools, tennis courts, golf courses and the charges, sports facilities, entertainment, hairdressing, valeting, theater tickets, and secretarial services.
- Details of facilities and equipment in the hotel for meetings, seminars, conventions, and other events.
- Information on all transport to and from airports, on bus and train timetables, airline schedules, car rental.
- Parking facilities at the hotel.
- Information on facilities for the elderly, handicapped, children, and pets.
- Information on special promotions and offers by the hotel for midweek reservations, weekend package deals, special programs for Christmas, Easter, Thanksgiving, and other holidays.
- Details of the types of menus offered by the hotel and the times of service.
- The entertainment program offered by the hotel.
- Information on local events, entertainment, and places of interest.
- Details of contacts with travel agents, tour operators, airlines, business organizations, and central reservations numbers with whom contact can be made if rooms become available.
- Rules relating to check-in and check-out times, methods of payment of accounts, and walk-in business.
- Any other specialized information regarding the establishment.

Every employee of an organization is a salesman of the company's product. In very large hotels the separate departments tend to become very insular, but the guests expect to get answers to their questions from any employee. It does not create a good impression if an employee cannot answer a simple question about, for example, the scheduling of live entertainment in the lounge.

To develop awareness and knowledge of the product they are selling, new employees should be given short training sessions where they have to answer simple questions such as the following:

1. Describe the layout of the room in the hotel used for seminars or meetings.

2. Name some of the items on the Sunday brunch menu and the prices.
3. What entertainment will be in the hotel's lounge bar during the next four weeks?
4. Does the hotel provide a playroom for children? If so describe the range of activities for children up to twelve years of age.
5. During what hours is the swimming instructor at the pool?
6. What is the maximum number of people that can be accommodated for a special banquet?

METHODS OF SELLING

Selling is done by telephone and in person almost every day. A good telephone voice is a considerable asset. Tone and manner will immediately create a favorable impression in the mind of the caller. When dealing with an inquiry, it is essential that all information about the establishment and its services are at hand. Nothing is more irritating to a caller than to be put on hold while information is retrieved. When someone is asking about room availability always have alternatives to offer if the caller's first choice is not available.

Selling is an art whether by telephone or face-to-face. A good selling technique can be developed so that with quiet confidence, knowledge, and enthusiasm for the product, the desk staff can highlight the special features of the establishment so that the potential guest feels that the hotel has something extra special to offer. Instead of just quoting bare facts about the rooms and facilities of the hotel, one can add small descriptive notes without exaggerating. For example:

Question: Where is the hotel located?
Answer: We are off exit 40, highway 75, very centrally located for all forms of entertainment and places of interest.
Question: Are there parking facilities?
Answer: Yes, we have plenty of parking spaces for all our guests.
Question: Do you have a pool?
Answer: Yes, a heated swimming pool and tennis courts.
Question: Are there some good eating places nearby?
Answer: Yes, but we also have an excellent restaurant and coffee shop in the hotel.

The list is endless and a good reception associate will seize every opportunity to sell the services of the hotel without overselling or appearing pushy.

SELLING TO THE BUSINESS PERSON

A large percentage of hotel business comes from business travelers. Many companies and organizations reserve rooms at certain hotels or motels on a year-round basis at the transient special or corporate rate. They use it not only for their own personnel but also to house business associates and clients.

When selling services to the business traveler, remember that the circumstances and their needs will be different than those of the vacationer or pleasure traveler.

1. Business people are usually traveling at the company's expense and are unlikely to be on a strict budget. They will probably require room service, including late night meals and beverages, and will avail themselves of the amenities of the hotel.
2. They are traveling out of necessity not for pleasure, therefore the hotel must be a home away from home. They will most likely eat in the hotel and use the lounge bars.
3. Time is usually of the essence to the business person; therefore, they will want quick, efficient check-in and check-out.
4. The rooms must have radio, television, direct dialing telephone, and a good flat surface on which to work at business papers.
5. Information must be readily available at the front desk on the area, the location of the nearest airport, the airline schedules, and any other matters the business person might need to know.
6. If the services are satisfactory the business people are likely to become regular guests of the hotel and recommend it to their associates.
7. There are no high or low seasons for the business traveler and they often require accommodation at short notice. Companies who use a hotel on a regular basis usually make the reservations for their representatives, and the account is sent direct to the company for settlement.

CONFERENCE AND GROUP BUSINESS

Annual surveys have shown that group business represents as much as 50 percent or more of the room pick-up at resorts. The types of corporate meetings held falls into the following categories:

Sales meetings
Annual meetings
Conventions
VIP and board meetings
Training meetings
Management meetings
Marketing meetings
Committee meetings
Educational seminars
Incentive travel
Product introductions
Other

This is a specialized market that grosses billions of dollars annually. It is increasingly competitive, and organizers, whose function it is to provide complete package deals for buyers, are constantly looking for new hotels that can offer something different.

It is not only the very large hotels who enter this market; medium-size hotels with good facilities can often accommodate the smaller trade exhibitions, training seminars, and meetings. Hotels wishing to attract this type of business must be able to put together composite package deals at competitive rates and offer them to the agencies that handle group business. To compete in this market, managers should:

1. Study what has been successfully marketed in the past.
2. Consider the size, structure, and special features of the establishment, and what type of event it could best manage—meetings, seminars, sports events, banquets.
3. Study the locality and its geographical, historical, or sporting interests. Are there beaches, good golf courses, boat marinas, good fishing, theaters, attractions, or other places of interest nearby.
4. Structure a group-business program, including sporting and entertainment, events for spouses, such as fashion shows, aerobic classes, tennis clinics.

Large Conferences and Meetings

Large hotels are comfortably geared to provide for any type and size of conference. They usually have a wide range of rooms available, with major conference and banqueting areas supplemented by smaller meeting rooms, private suites, and other facilities.

Hotels able to handle large group business have their own carefully prepared folders, sent to convention bureaus, group booking agencies, and consultants, describing the area and listing all the facilities they are able to offer. The front desk personnel must study this information so they are able to answer any questions on the following.

Dimensions of Rooms:
- floor area
- room length
- room width
- ceiling heights

Maximum Capacity of Each Room for:
- luncheon/dinner—round tables or sprigs (top table with branches)
- dinner dance
- cocktail reception
- fashion show
- stage show
- conference room only with school-room style set-up or cinema style set-up
- conference with breakfast/luncheon/dinner

Other Information:
- ventilation—air conditioning control
- sound insulation
- lighting equipment
- technological equipment—projectors, screens, sound
- access for loading and unloading equipment
- space for exhibition booths
- telephones
- switches and power points
- TV outlets—closed circuit
- microphones and audio jacks
- amplifiers
- movable partitions, chalkboards, flipboards

- clocks
- direct dialing services
- emergency exits
- total units of electricity available

Secretarial Services:
- telex
- photocopying
- printing of schedules, lists, speeches, name tags, menus
- translation service

Conference and Group Booking

When a booking is made, the management will discuss in full all the details and requirements, then prepare checklists with the organizers. When these are finalized and accepted, schedules will be prepared and put into action. Many details must be covered, and the following list presents only some of the actions that must be taken in preparing for a group.

1. Rooms will be assigned to VIPs, delegates and their spouses (if applicable), and organizers.
2. Meeting rooms and equipment required will be assigned, planned, and organized.
3. The front office manager will have a detailed schedule of estimated number of guests and other rooms required.
4. The food and beverage manager will be given a detailed schedule of meals required, and will discuss it with the executive chef.
5. The bars manager will be given a schedule of estimated number of guests expected.
6. The bell captain and head housekeeper will also have detailed schedules.

MARKETING

The term *marketing* gained prominence during the 1950s. Today the marketing executive is responsible for coordinating all aspects of a product or service: from packaging, labeling, and presenting the product in a manner likely to improve its salability, to exploiting the existing markets and creating new ones. Marketing a hotel involves several factors, from research to promotion and advertising.

Market Research and Analysis

Most states have a Division of Tourism, Office of Marketing Research that operates visitors' centers, conducts hospitality and courtesy programs, prepares and distributes travel literature, and promotes conventions, corporate meetings, and special events. Departments of Commerce have ongoing research programs investigating the impact of tourism on the state's economy and designing better ways to market their state as a tourist attraction. Survey programs are carried out and person-to-person interviews are conducted annually by professional interviewing staff. Travelers are asked to complete questionnaires that include questions on their choices of locale and accommodation.

Once the questionnaires are processed, the studies and statistics are made available to the hospitality and tourism industry, and any other interested parties, including the public.

Most hotels and the hotel industry in general also conduct market research into current market trends, statistics, and information contained in their own sales analysis reports, guests' record cards, guest history cards, and other statistics provided by the trade magazines.

Questionnaires in the rooms (fig. 4-1), inviting guests to comment on the standards in the hotel, are studied and analyzed. The replies and comments provide ideas on how to improve the salability of the product.

Promotional Literature

Brochures advertising the establishment should be well designed, colorful, and accurately descriptive. If the hotel is part of a group, literature on the other hotels within the group should be on display, and receptionists should be instructed to see they are distributed to guests and other inquirers.

Promotional Giveaways

Giveaway packs in the rooms are designed not only to create a welcoming impression in the guest's mind, but to advertise and pro-

PEACOCK LODGE

* * * *

To assist us in maintaining our high standards, we solicit your comments on our performance.

Please Check ✓

	Excellent	Good	Average	Poor

1 How did you make your reservation?
    By direct reservation
    Through central reservations				

2 How do you rate the following:
    Reception desk service
    Baggage handler's service
    Switchboard service
    TV reception
    Room cleanliness
    Room service				

3 How do you rate our food service?
    Quality of food
    Quality of service
    Menu selection
    Prices
    Cleanliness				

4 How do you rate our lounge?
    Quality of beverages
    Quality of service
    Prices
    Entertainment				

5 How do you rate the hotel facilities?				

6 What do you like most about our hotel? _____

7 What do you like least about our hotel? _____

8 Additional comments _____

Date	Room No.	Name and address (if you wish)

We thank you for staying with us and appreciate your comments. Please be assured they will be given every consideration – after all, we hope to see you again.

From the entire Peacock Lodge staff

4-1.   Typical market-research questionnaire.

mote the hotel. Giveaways such as matches, note pads, pens, pencils, diaries, calendars, and stationery can be considered a good investment if they promote a good image that the guest will remember and recommend.

Personal Selling

All members of staff, in particular the reception and contact personnel, must be trained in the development of selling techniques and good public relations work. They must know their product thoroughly and how to promote it by word-of-mouth, telephone, and correspondence. Staff should be involved in the marketing and sales programs, targets should be set and staff rewarded if goals are achieved.

Advertising

The method of advertising is a corporate or management decision and will depend largely on an advertising and marketing budget. Several different types of media are available from print media—national and local newspapers, trade magazines, guidebooks, national magazines—to billboards, radio, television, direct mail, and newsletters. The advertising and marketing executives will select the method that gives them the best coverage and results, within their financial means.

Travel Agents' and Tour Operators' Promotions

Colorful imaginative advertising programs are devised to promote package deals offered by tour operators. Airlines in conjunction with the hotels advertise cheap air travel and accommodation at certain hotels, especially during the low season.

Promoting Special Services and Events

Many hotels show enterprise and imagination in staging and promoting special events such as golf and fishing vacations, dude ranches, tennis tournaments, and many more. These types of events gain the hotel a reputation for offering something different.

Overseas Marketing

The United States Travel and Tourism Administration produces statistics on the number of international visitors each year and their value to the economy. Market analysis executives study these facts and figures and from the information therein plan their advertising campaigns to attract more foreign visitors. Anyone requiring information about a certain country can apply to the Foreign Tourist Bureau of that particular country. The offices are usually located in New York City.

Many planners and organizers of international conferences looking to select international sites for such events will expect answers to the following questions:

1. Does the hotel have a good range of conference facilities?
2. Is the hotel located near an international airport?
3. What are the climatic and seasonal factors of the area?
4. What cultural and recreational attractions are there in the area?
5. Are there transportation services available to the airport and major attractions in the area?
6. Does the hotel have adequate room capacity for the dates required?
7. Are the room rates within the budget of the organizer?
8. Are the management and staff trained to handle international conferences? Are there multilingual members of staff?
9. Is the food and beverage department able to meet the requests likely to come from foreign visitors?
10. Are medical and emergency services available?
11. Will secretarial and translation services be available?

The answers to these and many other questions likely to be asked will stem from the salespeople being thoroughly familiar and having full knowledge of the product they are selling, which is their hotel.

CHAPTER SUMMARY

"A room not sold for one night is a financial loss to an establishment that cannot be regained." This statement emphasizes the importance of the front desk personnel's role in selling the hotel's services. This chapter discusses different methods of selling, and the rules to be followed when selling accommodation. It highlights the importance of front desk personnel being thoroughly familiar with the product they are selling, which is the hotel, its services, and facilities.

Marketing is the long-range approach to business planning and involves finding out what the customers need or desire and selling it to them at a profit. This chapter gives an insight and understanding of how the hotel/motel industry is marketed.

Important points discussed are:

- Selling techniques
- The front desk reception area as a sales department
- Selling to the business person
- Selling to conference, meetings, travel, and group business agents
- Marketing, market research, and analysis
- Promotional literature, advertising, giveaways
- Promoting special services and events
- Overseas marketing

FOR DISCUSSION

1. Discuss why the techniques of selling accommodation by front desk personnel would be governed to some extent by the type of customer you are having to deal with.
2. Discuss the statement, "A satisfied guest will become a word-of-mouth salesman and promote the hotel."
3. Research a medium-size hotel in your area, and discuss how you would sell that particular product.
4. "Personal selling is an art whether by telephone or word-of-mouth." Discuss this statement.
5. Discuss how and why the needs of a business traveler differ from those of the vacationer or pleasure traveler.
6. Planners and organizers of conventions, conferences, meetings, group travel, and special functions are constantly looking for new hotels and venues that can offer something different every year. Discuss the importance of this specialized market to the hotel industry.
7. Discuss the importance of overseas marketing.
8. An organizer and planner of an international conference that will include foreign visitors from several different countries is researching your area to find a suitable hotel. Discuss the facilities he/she may be looking for.

KEY TERMS

The product
Selling techniques
Overselling
Face-to-face selling
Word-of-mouth selling
Business traveler
Corporate meetings
Educational seminars
Conventions
Conferences
Group travel
Marketing
Market research and analysis

CHAPTER QUIZ

1. What are the basic rules to be followed when selling accommodation from the reception desk?

2. Discuss the statement, "There is no substitute for knowledge." Relate it specifically to front desk personnel as salespeople.

3. Give five examples of using good sales techniques.

4. How do the methods of selling to a business person and a vacationer differ?

5. What essential information would need to be at hand when dealing with an inquiry from a conference organizer?

6. Define the term *marketing* and discuss all it implies.

7. What would you have to consider and what methods would you use if you were asked for promotional ideas for a newly built hotel?

5

BOOKKEEPING AND ACCOUNTING

BASIC PRINCIPLES OF DOUBLE-ENTRY BOOKKEEPING

Bookkeeping is the recording of business transactions, in a reliable manner, to provide a functional record and to meet federal and state statutory requirements and tax obligations. Bookkeeping also provides a business executive with records that will reveal: whether the business has made a profit or loss; how the profit or loss has been made; and what the financial position of the business is in terms of assets and liabilities.

Accounting calls for an in-depth understanding of business transactions and an ability to interpret and analyze the information provided by the bookkeeping system. Before students can progress to accounting and the interpretation of such financial statements as the income statement and the balance sheet, they should have a sound knowledge of the basic principles underlying the double-entry bookkeeping system.

Double Entry

The double-entry bookkeeping system (fig. 5-1), is based on the principle that for every business transaction that takes place **two** entries

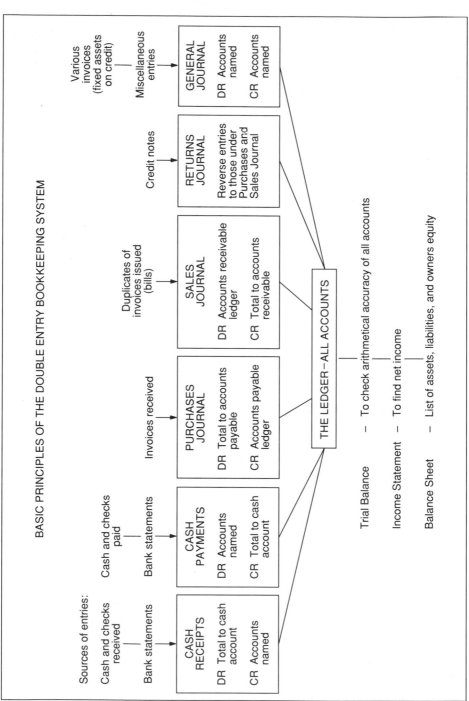

5-1 The double-entry bookkeeping system

must be made in the accounts: a **debit** entry (left side of an account page), showing merchandise or value coming into the business, and a corresponding **credit** entry (right side of an account), showing merchandise or value going out of the business.

Example 1
A hotel lets a room for a night, and the guest pays $50 cash for the night's lodging. The cash account would be **debited** (left-hand side) with $50 coming into the business. The sales account would be **credited** (right-hand side) with the $50 value of the room for the night, which went out of the business as a sale.

Example 2
The bar manager stocks up on $300 worth of liquor for the lounge bars. The purchases account would be **debited** (left-hand side) with $300 for merchandise in. The cash account would be **credited** (right-hand side) with a check for $300 going out as payment for the liquor.

Example 3
The hotel pays out $1000 in wages. The wages account is **debited** with $1000 being the cost of labor used in the business. The cash account is **credited** with $1000 going out as wages.
At any given time the total **debit** entries should equal the total **credit** entries, making it simple to check for arithmetical accuracy and locate errors. This is the main advantage of the double-entry bookkeeping system.

The Ledger

The principal book in the double-entry system is a ledger, the term used for a collection of accounts in which all business transactions are recorded, either individually or as totals posted from subsidiary books (figs. 5-2, 5-3).

BUSINESS DOCUMENTS

The basic business documents that are used for control purposes and as the sources of entries for the accounts system come in every size, shape, and color depending entirely on the requirements of the business that issues them.

Date	Particulars	Ref.	Debit		Credit		Balance	

LEDGER CARD   Number:

Peters, Bruce. Tallahassee, Florida

5-2.   Ledger card.

Purchase-Order Form

Whenever merchandise is required, an official purchase order form (fig. 5-4) should be sent to the supplier, giving details of the order, quoting the supplier's catalogue numbers wherever possible, and bearing

GENERAL LEDGER

CAPITAL – B. Jones   A/C 1

Date	Details	Ref.	Debit	Credit	Balance
June 1	Check 20			10,000.00	(10,000.00)

CASH/BANK   A/C 2

Date	Details	Ref.	Debit	Credit	Balance
June 30	Cash/Check Receipts	CR 1	12,158.00		12,158.00
30	Cash/Check Receipts	CP 1		1,089.57	11,068.43

PURCHASES   A/C 3

Date	Details	Ref.	Debit	Credit	Balance
June 30	Credit Purchases	PJ 1	756.00		756.00
30	Purchases Returns	PRJ1		99.50	656.50

SALES   A/C 4

Date	Details	Ref.	Debit	Credit	Balance
June 30	Cash Sales			2,060.00	2,060.00
30	Credit Sales			382.00	(2,442.00)

DISCOUNTS   A/C 5

Date	Details	Ref.	Debit	Credit	Balance
June 30	Discounts Allowed	CR 1	2.00		2.00
30	Discounts Received	CP 1		6.93	(4.93)

ACCOUNTS PAYABLE   A/C 6

Date	Details	Ref.	Debit	Credit	Balance
June 30	Total Balances	A/P		310.00	(310.00)

ACCOUNTS RECEIVABLE   A/C 7

Date	Details	Ref.	Debit	Credit	Balance
June 30	Total Balances	AR1	282.00		282.00

ICM Co.   Rent   A/C 8

Date	Details	Ref.	Debit	Credit	Balance
June 1	Check 101	CP 1	500.00		500.00

L.B. INSURANCE   A/C 9

Date	Details	Ref.	Debit	Credit	Balance
June 1	Check 102	CP 2	250.00		250.00

5-3. General ledger.

****PEACOCK LODGE****

Jamesville, Florida 34567

(813) 123-4567

Purchase Order   No. 333

To: ABC Suppliers Company   Date: June 1, 19--
    10 Sterry Street   Ship via: UPS
    Atlanta, Georgia 32301   Terms: 2/10 n/30

Cat. No.	Quantity	Size	Description	Price	Total
DCF 12	24	2 × 12	Twin Flat Blue Sheets	99.50	199.00
DCF 13	24	2 × 12	Twin Fitted Blue Sheets	87.50	175.00
DCF 40	48	2 × 24	Std. Blue Pillowcases	36.00	72.00

For Peacock Lodge by: (Signature)

5-4. Purchase order form.

the signature of an authorized person. Orders are usually numbered and in duplicate, triplicate, or as many copies as the business needs. The top copy goes to the supplier, and the others are retained for statistical purposes. Telephone orders should always be confirmed by an official order to save any arguments.

Delivery Ticket

Merchandise coming into the business should be accompanied by a delivery ticket showing details of merchandise supplies (fig. 5-5). The delivery ticket is for checking purposes. Any damages or shortages should be noted on the ticket before signing for acceptance of merchandise.

```
                    ABC SUPPLIERS COMPANY

                         10 Sterry Street
                      Atlanta, Georgia 32301

                       DELIVERY TICKET              No. 45
```

To: Peacock Lodge   Date: June 4, 19--
    Jamesville, Florida 34567   Ship via: UPS

	Cash	COD	Charge
			✓

Ref. No.	Quantity	Ctn. Size	Description	Price	Total
DCF 12	24	2 × 12	Twin Flat Blue Sheets		
DCF 13	24	2 × 12	Twin Fitted Blue Sheets		
DCF 40	48	2 × 24	Std. Blue Pillowcases		

Special Instructions:
    1 ctn. DCF 12 returned wrong color

Delivered by: (Signature)   Received by: (Signature)

5-5. Delivery ticket.

Invoice

An invoice is a detailed account of merchandise purchased (fig. 5-6). It is numbered and shows quantities, quality, prices, packing charges, and details of terms and discounts. It is sent by the seller to the customer and should be checked against the order form and delivery ticket. All prices and calculations should also be checked. If correct the invoice is entered into the purchases journal (fig. 5-11).

No. 123

ABC SUPPLIERS COMPANY

10 Sterry Street
Atlanta, Georgia 32301

INVOICE

To: Peacock Lodge   Date: June 6, 19--
    Jamesville, Florida 34567   Ship via: UPS

Your Order No: 333
Terms: 2/10   n/30

Ref. No.	Quantity	Ctn. Size	Description	Price	Total
DCF 12	24	2 × 12	Twin Flat Blue Sheets	99.50	199.00
DCF 13	24	2 × 12	Twin Fitted Blue Sheets	87.50	175.00
DCF 40	48	2 × 24	Std. Blue Pillowcases	36.00	72.00
					446.00
			Sales tax if applicable		
			Shipping and insurance if applicable		

5-6. Invoice.

Credit Memo

A credit memo is sent by the seller to the customer when merchandise has been returned or an overcharge has been made (fig. 5-7).
It is numbered and usually printed in red. It shows that the customer's
account has been credited with the amount involved. Credit memos are
entered in the purchases returns journal (fig. 5-12).

Debit Note

When there has been an undercharge on an invoice, the supplier
will send the customer a debit note for the amount involved. This acts

No. 12

ABC SUPPLIERS COMPANY

10 Sterry Street
Atlanta, Georgia 32301

CREDIT NOTE

To: Peacock Lodge   Date: June 15, 19--
    Jamesville, Florida 34567

Your account credited as follows:

Ref. No.	Quantity	Ctn. Size	Description	Price	Total
DCF 12	12	1 × 12	Twin Flat Sheets	99.50	99.50
			(Returned wrong color)		
			Less sales tax if applicable		

5-7. Credit memo.

as a supplementary invoice and, if correct, will be accepted and dealt
with in the same manner as an invoice.

Statement

With the mechanization of accounts, invoices and statements are
very often written simultaneously (fig. 5-8). This is a summarized
account sent to the customer showing the amount owing at the beginning of the period, plus the amounts of the invoices issued for merchandise supplied. Any credit memos, cash paid, and discounts allowed are
deducted. The final figure on the statement is the balance due. The
statement is checked against the suppliers account in the ledger and if
correct is passed for payment.

Date	Ref.	Details		Debit	Credit	Balance
		ABC SUPPLIERS COMPANY				
		10 Sterry Street				
		Atlanta, Georgia 32301				
		STATEMENT				
		Date: June 30, 19--				
June 1		Balance	b/fwd			200.00
5	Inv. 92	Goods		120.00		320.00
5		Check			190.00	130.00
		Discount			10.00	120.00
6	Inv. 123	Goods		446.00		566.00
15	Cr. Memo 12	Returned Goods			99.50	466.50
20	Inv. 202	Goods		150.00		716.50
Terms:	2/10 n/30				Amount due:	716.50

5-8. Statement.

Examples of Posting to a Ledger Account

Example 1: A Debtor's Account (fig. 5-9)

On 1 March a debtor who has an account with the Atlas Hotel owed the hotel $230. On 7 March he entertained business associates at the hotel; bill no. 216 amounting to $66 was posted to his account.

Date	Details	Ref.	Debit	Credit	Balance
	DEBTOR				
Mar. 1	Balance	b/fwd			230.00
7	Bill No. 216		66.00		296.00
8	Allowance			5.00	291.00
31	Check			207.00	
31	Discount 10%			23.00	61.00

5-9. A debtor's account.

On 8 March an allowance of $5 for an overcharge on wine was posted to his account. On 31 March a check for $207 was received in settlement of his 1 March balance after taking off a 10 percent discount allowed for $23.

Example 2: A Creditor's Account (fig. 5-10)
On 1 March, a creditor who is a supplier to the Atlas Hotel was owed a balance of $85 for merchandise supplied. On 3 March merchandise was received from the supplier; invoice no. 23 valued at $35 was posted to his account. On 5 March credit memo no. 19 valued at $5 for merchandise that had been returned was posted to the account. On 30 March a check for $83.30 was sent to the supplier in settlement of the 1 March balance, after taking a 2 percent discount of $1.70. This was posted to the account.

SUBSIDIARY BOOKS

It would be impossible to record all transactions directly into the ledger as the volume would be too great; therefore, subsidiary books—books of first entry—are opened, and the totals from these books are posted to the appropriate accounts in the ledger.

The purchases journal. Used to record all invoices for merchandise purchased on credit coming into the business (fig. 5-11).

Purchases returns journal. Used to record all credit memos from the suppliers reflecting merchandise returned or shortages (fig. 5-12).

Credit sales journal. Used to record all invoices for sales on credit (fig. 5-13).

Accounts payable ledger. Contains an account for every cred-

SOLUTION

CREDITOR

Date	Details	Ref.	Debit	Credit	Balance
Mar. 1	Balance	b/fwd			85.00
3	Goods Inv. 23			35.00	120.00
5	Credit memo 19		5.00		115.00
30	Check		83.30		
	Discount 2%		1.70		30.00

5-10. A creditor's account.

Date	Invoice No.	Account debited	A/C P. Ledger No.	Amount
June 1	147	Wilson Co.	W3	125.00
6	123	ABC Suppliers Co.	A5	446.00
12	41	Lane Co.	L2	135.00
22	82	Barton Co.	B4	50.00
		Total to Purchases A/C		756.00

5-11.   The purchases journal.

itor—suppliers or vendors to the business (fig. 5-14). The monthly total is posted to the accounts payable control account in the general ledger.

Accounts receivable ledger. Contains an account for every debtor—credit customer of the business (fig. 5-15). The monthly total is posted to the accounts receivable control account in the general ledger.

The journal. A book of prime entry used to record transactions of an extraordinary nature (fig. 5-16). Entries are made in chronological order and require an explanation. These may include (1) opening entries when starting a business, (2) the purchase or sale of fixed assets on credit, (3) correction of errors, (4) closing entries and transferring accounts, (5) miscellaneous entries that require explanation. A journal entry consists of three parts: (1) a debit entry; (2) a credit entry; (3) a brief note of explanation. These entries are transferred to accounts in the general ledger.

Date	Credit Memo	Account credited	A/C P. Ledger No.	Amount
June 15	12	ABC Suppliers Co.	A5	99.50
		Total to Purchases Returns		99.50
				GL 3

5-12.   The purchases returns journal.

Date	Invoice No.	Account credited	A/C R. Ledger No.	Amount
June 2	101	Horton Co.	H2	62.00
8	102	Masson Co.	M4	100.00
16	103	Crown Co.	C8	88.00
24	104	James Co.	J3	132.00
		Total to Sales A/C		382.00
				GL 4

5-13. Credit sales journal.

ABC Suppliers Co.   A/C   A5

Date	Details	Ref.	Debit	Credit	Balance
June 6	Invoice 123	PJ 1		446.00	446.00
15	Credit Memo	PRJ1	99.50		346.50
20	Check 103		339.57		6.93
20	Discount		6.93		00.00

BARTON Co.   A/C   B4

Date	Details	Ref.	Debit	Credit	Balance
June 22	Invoice 82	PJ 1		50.00	50.00

LANE Co.   A/C   L2

Date	Details	Ref.	Debit	Credit	Balance
June 12	Invoice 41	PJ 1		135.00	135.00

WILSON Co.   A/C   W3

Date	Details	Ref.	Debit	Credit	Balance
June 1	Invoice 147	PJ 1		125.00	125.00

5-14. Accounts payable subsidiary ledger.

CROWN CO.   A/C   C.8

Date	Details	Ref.	Debit	Credit	Balance
June 16	Invoice 103	SJ. 1	88.00		88.00

HORTON CO.   A/C   H.2

Date	Details	Ref.	Debit	Credit	Balance
June 2	Invoice 101	SJ. 1	62.00		62.00

JAMES CO.   A/C   J.3

Date	Details	Ref.	Debit	Credit	Balance
June 24	Invoice 104	SJ. 1	132.00		132.00

WILSON Co.   A/C   M.4

Date	Details	Ref.	Debit	Credit	Balance
June 8	Invoice 102	SJ. 1	100.00		100.00
30	Check			98.00	
	Discount			2.00	00.00

5-15. Accounts receivable subsidiary ledger.

GENERAL JOURNAL

Date	Details	Ref.	Debit	Credit
June 1	Restaurant Furniture A/C Martin Furniture Co. Purchased New Restaurant Furniture – Inv. 320	G.L.F.1. GL M6	1500.00	1500.00

5-16. The journal.

Date	Account To Be Credited	Ref.	Total	Cash Sales	Discounts Allowed
June 1	Capital B. Jones	GL. 1	10,000.00		
1	Cash Sales		400.00	400.00	
7	Cash Sales		360.00	360.00	
15	Cash Sales		600.00	600.00	
22	Cash Sales		275.00	275.00	
30	Cash Sales		425.00	425.00	
30	Masson Co.	A/c R M4	98.00		2.00
			12,158.00	2,060.00	2.00
			GL. 2	Sales GL. 4	GL. 5

CASH RECEIPTS JOURNAL — Page 1

5-17. The cash receipts journal.

Cash Receipts and Cash Payments Journals

Whether the accounting system of the establishment is mechanized or manual, the basic principles of recording cash receipts and cash payments remain the same (figs. 5-17, 5-18). Cash and checks received will be **debited** (left-hand side) in the cash book; cash and checks paid

Date	Account To Be Debited	Check No.	Ref.	Total	Discounts Received
June 1	ICM Co. – Rent	101	GL. 8	500.00	
5	LB Insurance	102	GL. 9	250.00	
20	ABC Supplies Co.	103	A/R A5	339.57	6.93
				1089.57	6.93
				GL. 2	GL. 5

CASH PAYMENTS JOURNAL — Page 1

5-18. The cash payments journal.

out will be **credited** (right-hand side) in the cash book. Entries are then posted to the appropriate accounts in the general ledger.

The following example will illustrate the principle of the double-entry bookkeeping system. The transactions are recorded in figures 5-3, and 5-11 through 5-19.

Date	Transaction
6/1	Mr B. Jones started a business with $10,000 cash as capital which he placed in a bank account
6/1	Bought merchandise on credit from Wilson Co. $125
6/1	Cash sales $400
6/1	Paid $500 to ICM Co. for rent
6/2	Sold merchandise on credit to Horton Co., $62
6/5	Paid $250 to L. B. Insurance
6/6	Bought merchandise on credit from ABC suppliers, $446.
6/7	Cash sales, $360
6/8	Sold merchandise on credit to Masson Co., $100
6/12	Bought merchandise on credit from Lane Co., $135
6/15	Received a credit memo from ABC Suppliers, $99.50
6/15	Cash sales, $600
6/16	Sold merchandise on credit to Crown Co., $88
6/20	Paid ABC Suppliers, $339.57, receiving $6.93 discount
6/22	Cash sales, $275
6/22	Bought merchandise on credit from Barton Co., $50
6/24	Sold merchandise on credit to James Co., $132
6/30	Cash sales, $425
6/30	Received check from Masson Co. for $98, allowing them a $2 discount (settlement of their account)

THE TRIAL BALANCE

The trial balance is a list of the balances extracted from the general ledger at the conclusion of posting (fig. 5-19). It provides a check on the arithmetical accuracy of the double-entry, but it is not proof that the transactions have been correctly recorded.

Some of the errors a trial balance will show include the following:

- Cash book balanced incorrectly
- Incorrect additions of sales, purchases, or returns journals
- Entry posted to the wrong side of an account
- Incorrect amount posted to the ledger

TRIAL BALANCE as at 30 June 1988			
Account	Folio No.	Debit	Credit
Capital – B. Jones	1		10,000.00
Cash/Bank	2	11,068.43	
Purchases	3	656.50	
Sales	4		2,442.00
Discounts	5		4.93
Accounts Payable	6		310.00
Accounts Receivable	7	282.00	
ICM Rent	8	500.00	
LB Insurance	9	250.00	
		12,756.93	12,756.93

5-19. The trial balance.

- Discounts transferred incorrectly
- A debit or credit omitted in posting

Some of the errors a trial balance will not show include:

- error of omission—An entry completely omitted from all journals.
- error of commission—Entry posted to the wrong account.
- error of principle—A purchase treated as a sale, a receipt treated as a payment, returns in treated as returns out, an asset treated as an expense.
- error in original entry—Wrong amount entered in the journal of first entry.
- compensating error—Two errors of the same amount, one on debited side of the ledger, one on the credit side.
- error of duplication—The same transaction entered twice.

Errors can be located in a trial balance by following a step-by-step procedure:

1. Check the general ledger to see if every account, including the cash and bank account, is in the trial balance.
2. Check the balance of the cash book.

3. Check all totals in subsidiary journals of first entry.
4. Find the difference between the trial balance debit and credit totals, halve the difference, and look for this amount which may have been posted to the wrong side.
5. Check the balances of the ledger accounts for accuracy.
6. Check all folio columns for an omission in posting.
7. Check each item in the ledger against the journal of first entry.
8. Look for "slides," for example, $17.99 written as $71.99.

CONTROL ACCOUNTS

A control account is constructed apart from the system of the double-entry. It is a device that enables a check to be made on accounts receivable and accounts payable sections of the general ledger. The total balances of the accounts receivable will give the total "debtors." The total balances of the accounts payable will give the total "creditors." (Figures 5-20 and 5-21 show manual bookkeeping.) One of the advantages of computerized accounting is that the amounts of the individual postings each day can be accumulated so that the total balance of the ledgers can be ascertained daily.

THE PETTY CASH JOURNAL

Petty cash must not be confused with the cash floats that are the fixed sums of money handed out to various departments such

Debit			Credit		
Date	Detail	Amount	Date	Detail	Amount
Jan. 31	Allowances	20.00	Jan. 1	Total Balances	572.00
31	Cash/Checks and		31	Total Sales	482.00
	Discounts	250.00			
31	Balances c/d	784.00			
		1054.00			1054.00
			Feb. 1	Total Balances b/d	784.00

NOTE: b/d = brought down
      c/d = carried down

5-20. The accounts receivable control account.

Debit			Credit		
Date	Detail	Amount	Date	Detail	Amount
Jan. 1 31	Total Balances Total Purchases	400.00 570.00	Jan. 31 31 31	Purchases Returns Cash/Checks and Discounts Balances c/d	30.00 320.00 620.00
		970.00			970.00
Feb. 1	Total Balances b/d	620.00			

5-21. The accounts payable control account.

as the restaurants and lounges so that they have change available to start the day's business. Most businesses have a petty cash journal in which all small items of expenditure are recorded (fig. 5-22). The safest method of keeping control of petty cash is the "imprest" system whereby a petty cashier is entrusted with a fixed sum of money—the "imprest"—out of which all small payments are made. A petty cash book is kept showing to which account in the general ledger the totals will be posted. Periodically the petty cashier will present to the chief cashier for audit the petty cash book and signed vouchers for money handed out. The petty cashier will then receive a reimbursement which will bring the petty cash float up to the original imprest.

The imprest system has many advantages, including the following:

- The amount that can be embezzled is limited to the amount of the imprest.
- All small items are kept out of the main cash book.
- Small items of expenditure can be analyzed and controlled. This is important as they can mount up over a period of time.
- There is a regular audit on petty cash expenditure.
- The petty cashier has to account for the imprest and expenditure of the petty cash.

THE GUEST TABULAR LEDGER

In hotel and catering accounts, the sales journal is replaced by a guest ledger containing the accounts of people staying at the hotel, and a city ledger for the credit accounts of businessmen and others. The

PETTY CASH BOOK

Cash Float	Date	Details	Voucher No.	Total	Office Supplies	Postage Expenses	Magazines	Florist	Tips	Charity (Paid Out)	Sundry Expenses	Paid Out for Guests	Posted to Guest's Bill
50.00	1988 Jan 1	Cash Float (Imprest)		— —									
	2	Florist	1	20.00				20.00					
	3	Plants	2	5.00				5.00					
	3	Taxi Mrs. White Rm. 201	3	7.00								7.00	Rm. 401
	3	Magazines	4	4.00			4.00						
	4	Office Supplies	5	6.50	6.50								
	5	Tip	6	1.00					1.00				
	6	Parcel	7	3.70		3.70							
	6	Charity	8	1.00						1.00			
	7	Extra Postage	9	.50		.50							
				48.70	6.50	4.20	4.00	25.00	1.00	1.00		7.00	
50.00		Balance	c/d	1.30									
				50.00									
1.30	7	Balance	b/d	— —									
48.70		Reimbursing Check		— —									

5-22. The petty cash journal.

118

guest tabular ledger (fig. 5-23) illustrates the principle of tabulation as control in a manually operated system. It is the same basic principle that underlies the computerized hotel lodging systems.

In the sample of a vertical guest tabular ledger page in figure 5-23 there are seventeen lines. The data, line-by-line, are as follows:

1. Room number
2. Room type
3. Name of guest
4. Balance brought forward from previous day
5. Room rate
6. Coffee shop—charge for breakfast, snacks
7. Luncheon—charge for luncheon taken in restaurant
8. Dinner—charge for dinner taken in restaurant
9. Room service—charge for any room service
10. Telephone—charge for telephone calls
11. Valet—charge for valet service
12. Newspapers—charge for newspapers, magazines
13. Sundry items—charges for sundries
14. Total debits—total of all charges made to guest bill (folio) (nos. 4 through 14)
15. Cash/charge—any cash, check, or credit-card payment made
16. Balance carried forward—amount carried forward to next day's guest tabular ledger
17. Total credits—totals of all payments and balances carried forward

Sales tax is included and extracted from bills. A guest tabular ledger is made out for each day. To balance all columns should be added down and across and the total debits should equal the total credits, thus control is kept over each day's business.

Summary Sheets

Summary sheets are completed either weekly or monthly. Figure 5-24 illustrates a summary sheet from a hotel that offers meal plans with their accommodation.

BANKING

Virtually every business needs either one or more checking accounts. To open a checking account the bank requires a signature or signatures from the people authorized to sign checks on behalf of the

Page 2

GUEST TABULAR LEDGER

Date: June 1, 19 – –

1	Room No.	201	202	203	204	205	206	207	208	209	210	
2	Room Type	STD	STD	STD	STD	SUITE	Q	KL	K	STD	STD	
3	Name of Guest / Number of Guests	James 1	Walters 2	Sales 2	De Car 1	Stevens 4	Lanza 4	Lotto 2	Pfeffer 2	Biedes 1	Tollyen 1	Daily Total
4	Balance b/fwd	75.00	120.00	80.00	65.00	300.00	120.00	95.00	85.00	65.00	65.00	1070.00
5	Room Rate	65.00	65.00	65.00	65.00	125.00	75.00	95.00	85.00	65.00	65.00	770.00
6	Coffee Shop	3.75	7.50	7.50			16.00		7.50			42.25
7	Luncheon	5.25			6.50			15.00	22.00			48.75
8	Dinner		22.00	25.00		45.00	55.00			8.50	7.50	163.00
9	Room Service				5.00	21.00		18.00				44.00
10	Telephone	1.25		3.00		7.50				1.20		12.95
11	Valet					6.00		10.00				16.00
12	Newspapers	.75				.75	.75	.75				3.00
13	Sundry Items					5.00 (Flowers)						5.00
14	Total Debits	151.00	214.50	180.50	141.50	510.25	266.75	233.75	199.50	139.70	137.50	2174.95
15	Cash/Charge	151.00 AE			141.50 V	510.25 AE		233.75 MC			137.50 Cash	1174.00
16	Balance c/fwd		214.50	180.50			266.75		199.50	139.70		1000.95
17	Total Credits	151.00	214.50	180.50	141.50	510.25	266.75	233.75	199.50	139.70	137.50	2174.95

Note: Charges shown include sales tax.
b/fwd = brought forward
c/fwd = carried forward

5-23. The guest tabular ledger (manual).

WEEKLY SALES SUMMARY SHEET

Date	Rooms	AP	MAP	BP	CP	Wines	Room Service	Bars	Telephone	Valet	Vending Machine	Total	Allowance	Net Total
June 1		$	$	$	$	$	$	$	$	$	$	$	$	$
2														
3														
4														
5														
6														
7														
1	2	3	4	5	6	7	8	9	10	11	12	13	14	15

The total of columns 3–12 should add up to the total of column 13.
Allowances (14) should be taken away from total (13) to give net total (15).

5-24. Weekly summary report.

business. Books of checks and deposit slips are provided at a charge by the bank. Checks are imprinted with the name and address of the business, and the telephone number if required. An identification number is assigned by the bank to the account. This number is also printed on checks and deposit slips in magnetic ink so that transactions are automatically processed by computer. All checks are given a serial number, essential for internal accounting control.

To some extent, a hotel acts as a bank for its guests, primarily by cashing checks and traveler's checks, or accepting them as payment.

Accepting a Check

A cashier accepting a check from a guest should note the following points:

- The check must not exceed the limit set by management unless special authorization comes from the front desk manager.
- The date must be correct.
- The words and figures must agree; if either has been altered the alteration must be signed by the drawer.
- The hotel must be named as the payee.
- The guest must sign the check.
- Identification such as a driver's license and major credit card must be presented with the check.

There are several banking terms with which every front desk associate should be familiar:

Stop-payment orders. Checks can be lost or stolen, a preauthorized debit may have to be cancelled, or payment stopped on a check issued. In any of these events the bank must be notified immediately, quoting the check number and amount, and putting a stop payment on the check. The bank usually makes a charge for this service.

NSF checks (not sufficient funds). A check from a guest may bounce and be returned marked NSF, meaning simply that there were not sufficient funds in the drawer's account to meet the check. On receipt of an NSF check the accounts department must make a journal entry crediting the cash account and debiting accounts receivable of whomever issued the check. Appropriate action is taken against the person issuing the check.

Deposits. Deposit slips are usually in duplicate, the top copy for the bank, the second copy remains in the book as documentary proof of deposit. Checks are listed either by their bank code number or name on the reverse side and the total is entered on the front of a deposit slip along with any cash being deposited.

Bank statement. A bank statement is a detailed and summarized statement of the customer's account at the bank. It shows withdrawals, deposits, interest earned, and any service charges. It is usually sent out once a month and the customer has to reconcile it with his or her own cash book.

Bank reconciliation statement. In theory, the balance shown on a bank statement from the bank should agree with the balance in the cash book of the customer. This rarely happens, because (1) checks credited in the cash book may not have been presented to the bank for payment; (2) checks debited in the cash book may not have been deposited and credited by the bank before the bank statement was sent to the customer; (3) items on the bank statement such as service charges, preauthorized debits, interest credited, and loan charges have not been entered in the cash book.

To Reconcile the Bank Statement with the Cash Book

1. Check off all items that appear on both the bank statement and in the cash book, putting a cross by those items which do not appear in both.
2. Enter into the cash book those items that appear on the bank statement but not in the cash book, such as service charges, interest earned, or stop payment charges.
3. Balance the cash book and prepare a bank reconciliation statement.

CREDIT CARDS

Payment by credit card is often preferred by hotels and other businesses. The magnitude of the credit card business is illustrated by the statistics issued by one of the major credit card organizations (with permission of Visa International).

- Visa Classic and Premier cards are issued by nearly 17,000 financial institutions.
- The latest statistics indicate over 140 million Visa cards are in circulation around the world.
- Over $100 billion in transaction volume was conducted on Visa cards in 1985.
- Over 5.0 million merchants around the world accept Visa cards.

The other major credit card organizations, such as MasterCard and American Express, are certainly able to quote equally impressive figures. Diners Club and Carte Blanche have more than 5 million card-members worldwide.

Accepting Payment by Credit Card

When a guest checks-in at a hotel, he or she usually indicates whether payment will be made by credit card. If this is the case the cashier follows a set procedure:

1. Request the credit card from the guest, check the expiration date, make an imprint of the card on the sales voucher, and ask the guest to sign the voucher. This is checked against the signature on the card and also provides a signature against which any other sales vouchers, such as restaurant and bar bills, can be checked.
2. Major credit card companies have direct communication links either with the hotel's computer terminals or by telephone. By quoting the credit card number an approval or disapproval code will be given.
3. The sales voucher is in triplicate, one copy for the guest, the other two copies for the accounting procedures. When completing the charge record, make sure the correct date is on the imprinter; write clearly the amount, taxes, and total of the charge transaction. (If applicable have the card member fill in tip and total restaurant charge.) Always check the signature against the signature on the back of the card.

Security Systems

Most of the major credit card companies make available to the establishments who will honor their credit cards a simplified operations guide on how to handle credit card transactions, and the security measures that will provide protection against fraud, misrepresentation, and bookkeeping errors. In general, the following guidelines should be used.

- Check warning bulletins listing lost, stolen, or invalid cards whenever credit cards are offered for payment.
- Do not exceed the authorized floor limit that is set by the hotel. If a charge exceeds it, staff must obtain authorization.
- Use the approval or disapproval code-number system—either by computer hookup or telephone.
- If authorization is denied you will be advised not to honor the card. If you are suspicious about the person presenting the card, contact the company giving the code number for such circumstances, and you will be advised on procedure.

Accounting for Payment by Credit Card

Credit card companies operate on a commission basis. Sales vouchers for payment made by the bank credit cards are treated as cash. The vouchers are deposited into the bank on a separate deposit slip and the hotel account is credited with the amount less the credit card company's commission.

Sales vouchers relating to other credit card companies, such as American Express, Diners Club International, Carte Blanche, are dealt with in a different manner. Once charge summary sheets are prepared (in duplicate) the sales vouchers are listed and the hard copies of the vouchers and the summary sheet are sent to the credit card company at least once a week. The company will then pay the amount owing less commission direct to the establishment. In the accounts system, the cash and the discount received from credit card sales would be **debited** in the cash receipts journal and **credited** to the sales account.

TRAVELER'S CHECKS

Traveler's checks can be obtained from a bank or travel agency and are usually issued either in the currency of the home country of the traveler or the currency of the country being visited. Traveler's checks must be signed once in front of the person issuing them and again when they are presented as payment. The two signatures must correspond before they are acceptable. Proper identification is also requested. Lists of stolen or lost traveler's checks are circulated to hotels and should be consulted.

Foreign Currencies

Some major hotels can act as authorized agents for changing foreign currency. The cashier should observe the currency regulations and be aware of the rates of exchange, which change daily. Foreign currency is exchanged at a bank and any "profit of exchange" the hotel makes is entered in the cash received journal. Hotel reception desk personnel should be familiar with foreign currencies and how to convert them. For example, to convert two hundred English pounds into dollars find the current exchange rate, which will tell you what one pound equals in dollars, and multiply this by two hundred:

$$\text{Rate: } \$1.48 = £1$$
$$£200 \times 1.48 = \$296$$

Conversely, to change dollars into pounds, divide the amount of dollars by the same rate:

$$\$296 \text{ into English Pounds: } \frac{296}{1.48} = £200$$

MECHANIZED AND COMPUTERIZED ACCOUNTING SYSTEMS

The Advantages of Office Machines

1. Increased speed
2. Greater accuracy
3. Improved records
4. Elimination of tedious repetitive work
5. Information for management quickly and easily produced

Types of Office Accounting Machines

1. Adding machines
2. Calculating machines
3. Accounting/bookkeeping machines that perform numerous functions

Computerized Hotel Accounting Systems

Information technology (IT) has been defined as the use of computers, microelectronics, and telecommunications designed to help us produce, store, obtain, and send information in the form of pictures, words, or numbers more reliably, quickly, and economically. Without doubt, information technology has become the most rapidly developing area of business activity in the Western world. Certain basic terminology should be understood.

Hardware. The physical components of computers, including minicomputers, microcomputers, and integrated systems and attachments to the computers.

Software. Computer programs, including specially designed programs on various types of disk, for example, hard disks or floppy disks, which are used in conjunction with the hardware.

Floppy disk. A flexible disk. The surface should not be touched and it must be stored in a cool, dry place away from electrical equipment because it is magnetic.

Hard Disk. It is not possible to remove a hard disk. It is sealed and spins at very high speeds, and can therefore retrieve and store information very quickly.

As the hotel and catering industry continues to expand and develop internationally, there has grown a corresponding need for improved communications and services that provide up-to-the-minute information on the availability of accommodation and complete management control over complex accounting. The development of sophisticated computerized hotel accounting systems has become a highly competitive field.

It is not possible to go into the details of all the computerized systems on the market, but to name just a few used in the industry there are the NCR series (fig. 5-25), the Sweda International electronic cash registers, and the Hoskyns hotel accounting systems.

NCR Modular Lodging System (MLS)
(With permission of NCR International)

The keyboard of the NCR 7900 terminal includes a standard typewriter keyboard. Ten function keys enable up to twenty function codes to be transmitted to the processor for system control. The complete

5–25. A front desk associate at the terminal of a computerized hotel accounting system (Courtesy of NCR Corporation).

modular flexible control system covers every aspects of hotel management from reservations to check-out.

External Subsystems

External subsystems that are interfaced with MLS include

1. The hotel billing information center system (HOBICS) which provides telephone charge billing information for automatic posting to the guest folio.
2. The bar/restaurant system which enables posting charges from the hotel's bar and restaurant direct to the guest folios and charge account files.
3. The maid dial-in system which is used to allow maids to enter room status codes from push-button (only) phones in each guest room to update housekeeping records in the central data file.

MLS Reservations Application

1. Availability: Information on room availability for the current day and future dates can be examined.
2. Reservation entry: The operator can enter four types of reservations into the central data file.
    a. Guaranteed
    b. Nonguaranteed
    c. Standby
    d. Tentative
3. Room blocking: The system can:
    a. Find rooms available for blocking.
    b. Find suites available for blocking.
    c. Display blocked rooms.
    d. View the overall room rack.
    e. View the overbook screen to check availability.
4. Rate display: The rate display screen will show room rates for each type of room, by date, for the dates of stay and the number of children and adults.
5. Overbook minimum house available: The overbook minimum house available screen indicates when no rooms of a specific type are available on a specific date, and permits additional reservations up to the management-stated overbook limit. A password is required to exceed the overbook limit.
6. Group functions: Specialized processing facilitates the entry and maintenance of reservations for groups.
7. Deposit functions: Deposits can be entered and posted to reservations before registration. A report on deposit balance information is stored in the system and can be brought to the display screen.

The reservations application of MLS provides numerous reports from which the hotel management can select specific reports to be produced each day.

Registration and Rooms Management (RRM)

RRM is divided into four functional areas:

1. Registration
2. Rooms management
3. End-of-day
4. Management reports

Registration

Three types of guest can be registered.

1. Walk-ins
2. Individuals who have a registration
3. Groups who have a registration
   a. Conventions when group members arrive individually.
   b. Tour groups who usually arrive as a group.

Walk-in registration. Enter the guest's accommodation requirements, determine room availability, assign room number, and
register the guest.

Guests with reservations. Locate the reservation, assign a room
number, and register the guest.

Group registration. Locate the group reservation in the system's
file, register the entire group if a rooming list was made for
the reservation.

Rooms Management

The rooms management functions provide the information to
enable the lodging establishment to manage its inventory of salable
rooms. Each function is accessed through the function key of the same
name except maid dial-in which does not use a function key.

1. Room information
2. Room status
3. Guest select (used to up-date information about registered
   guests)
4. Phone select (used to enter specific guest data from an incoming telephone call in order to locate the guest and to connect
   the call)
5. Maid dial-in

A wide variety of registration and rooms management reports can be
produced from which the hotel management may select.

Guest Accounting Application

This system processes guest accounts from check-in through
check-out. The following functions are provided:

1. Create an account
2. Post account
3. Check-out
4. Special functions which include
    a. Starting the end-of-day processing
    b. Selecting certain accounting reports for printing
    c. Checking a guest's account balance and available credit
    d. Starting automatic posting
    e. Generating a cashier shift report
    f. Resetting daily revenue totals without resetting period-to-date totals

Summary

Computerized systems perform functions too numerous to list, but most are easy to operate, and easy to learn. Hotel personnel with no prior knowledge of computer operations can perform the following tasks on the computer with little training:

- Reserve rooms for individuals or groups
- Check availability for reservations or registration
- Register individual guests or groups
- Service inquiries regarding a reservation or registration
- Control status of individual rooms
- Update housekeeping status
- Post guest charges to folios
- Check-out guests
- Print end-of-day reports

Sweda (with Permission of Sweda International)

The Sweda is an electronic hotel posting machine and cash register that has been specially tailored for the hotel industry. It produces clear legible bills for the guest; fast accurate operations for reception; security and information for management.

It includes the following special features:

- Departmental digits that cover all services, such as valeting, telephone, restaurant, bars, coffeeshops
- Keys that cover all types of payment, including major credit cards

- Cashier totals
- Room balances
- Currency conversions
- Trial balance to facilitate hotel accounting
- A training mode for cashier training

Abbreviations Used in Machine Accounting

#. Number
AD. Advance deposit
BAL. Balance, or balance key
C. Bal. Credit balance
CID. Cash in drawer
C/L. City ledger
Comp. Complimentary, or compulsory
D. BAL. Debit balance
Dept. Department
IRC. Interregister communications
MAX. Maximum
MIN. Minimum
P. BAL. Previous balance
PLU. Price lookup
ROOM #. Room pickup key
S. TL. Subtotal

CHAPTER SUMMARY

This chapter describes bookkeeping and accounting procedures. It deals with the basic principles and practices underlying the double-entry bookkeeping system, whether it be manually operated or computerized.

Important points and topics discussed are:

- Double-entry bookkeeping system
- Business documents
- Ledger accounts
- Subsidiary journals
- Cash receipts and cash payments

- Trial balance
- Control accounts
- Manual guest tabular ledger
- Banking
- Credit cards
- Computerized hotel accounting systems

FOR DISCUSSION

1. "Many businesses fail because of inefficient bookkeeping and accounting systems and inadequate records." Discuss this statement.
2. "Credit cards are now more acceptable than cash or check when settling an account." Discuss the reasons for this trend.
3. Compare manual and computerized bookkeeping systems, and discuss the advantages and disadvantages of both systems.
4. Discuss why it is important that a basic knowledge of the principles and practices of the double-entry bookkeeping system is essential even though the accounting system is fully computerized.
5. Research and discuss federal and state statutory requirements and tax obligations in relation to operating a hotel/motel.

KEY TERMS

Debit
Credit
Debtor
Creditor
Ledger
Invoice
Statement
Accounts payable
Accounts receivable
Cash receipts
Cash payments
Petty cash
Preauthorized debit

Deposits
Bank statement
Bank reconciliation
Hardware
Software
Floppy disk
Hard disk
The trial balance
Control account
Guest's account (folio)
NSF checks

CHAPTER QUIZ

1. Define the terms *bookkeeping* and *accounting*.

2. Explain briefly the principle of the double-entry bookkeeping system and its advantages.

3. Name the subsidiary journals in the accounting system and their purposes.

4. J. Chalan is a supplier to the Peacock Lodge. From the following information, create an account, and complete and post the transactions onto his ledger card in the hotel's accounts.

Date	Transaction	Amount
Mar. 1.	Balance owing to J. Chalan.	$172
Mar. 2.	Merchandise supplied by J. Chalan, Inv. 326	135
Mar. 3.	Check sent to J. Chalan in settlement of balance owing Mar. 1, less 5% discount	
Mar. 4.	Credit memo received from J. Chalan	23
Mar. 4.	Merchandise supplied by J. Chalan, Inv. 420	141
Mar. 5.	Balance the account	

5. From the following information, prepare a bank reconciliation statement as at 31 March 1987.

   The bank statement shows a credit balance of $1298
   Checks drawn but not yet presented for payment = $131
   Preauthorized payments not shown in cash journal = $82
   Checks entered in cash journal but not yet paid into bank = $564.

   What would the cash journal balance show?

6. Define the following:
   a. Error of omission
   b. Error of duplication
   c. Error of original entry
   d. Compensating error
   e. Error of principle
   f. Error of commission

7. What procedures should a cashier follow when accepting a check-in settlement of an account from a guest?

8. What are the standard procedures to follow when a guest indicates he or she will settle his or her account by credit card?

9. What do you understand by the "imprest" system of keeping petty cash? What are its advantages?

10. What do the following computer terms mean:
    a. Hardware
    b. Software
    c. Hard disk
    d. Floppy disk

11. What do the following abbreviations used in machine accounting mean?
    a. AD
    b. C BAL
    c. C/L
    d. PLU
    e. Comp
    f. D BAL

g. IRC
h. P. BAL
i. CID
j. S. TL

12. Summarize some of the main operations that can be performed by a computerized hotel accounting system.

6

BUSINESS PRACTICE

In large hotels for transients where the length of stay of the guests averages only two to three nights, the volume of work will probably result in a high degree of specialization, and the tasks performed by front office personnel will be subdivided. In such hotels, the brigade of reception personnel would be occupied largely with front desk reception duties, connected with selling accommodation. In smaller establishments—such as motor lodges, motor inns, motels, and medium-size hotels—all the office work will be centralized in the front office, and during quiet periods, the front desk clerks would be expected to carry out the tasks of maintaining accounting and other records.

However, whether employed in a large, medium, or small establishment, the front office personnel should have a sound knowledge of general business practices and, if called upon to do so, should be able to perform competently and efficiently the following tasks:

- Deal with correspondence
- Handle ingoing and outgoing mail
- Control of stationery
- File and maintain records
- Photocopy
- Maintain inventory-control systems
- Maintain payroll and staff records
- Prepare statistics and reports

CORRESPONDENCE

Every business letter should be written with the idea of creating a favorable impression in the mind of the reader. A badly constructed letter, crude in style, vague in wording and careless in grammar, will create an unfavorable impression, whereas a well-framed letter, clear and concise in wording, indicates efficiency.

To be an effective correspondent, one should have a good grasp of the rules governing spelling, grammar, and punctuation, and also be able to construct sentences so that the exact meaning is conveyed in the fewest possible words. Business terms, definitions, and abbreviations should be studied and understood.

Desirable Features of a Good Business Letter

Accuracy. As business letters are usually records of business transactions, all details must be scrupulously accurate.

Conciseness. The message of the letter must be conveyed in as few words as possible, using clear, simple expressions and avoiding the use of any unnecessary phrases.

Grammatical correctness. In addition to correct spelling, a sound knowledge of the rules of English grammar is essential. It is worth remembering that simple sentences are more likely to be grammatically correct than long, involved ones.

Courtesy. A business letter is often used to obtain new business or to create goodwill. Every letter should convey genuine sincerity and courtesy.

Presentation. The letter should present an attractive appearance and arrangement. A good letter-writer will place in a logical sequence the matter about which he or she intends to write. Each topic should be dealt with in a separate paragraph as paragraphing focuses attention on the important points in the correct order.

INCOMING MAIL

Business letters and inquiries for the attention of the management or heads of sections should be date-stamped, sorted, and distributed to the appropriate department immediately upon arrival.

Mail for Guests in Residence

Any incoming mail for guests should be sorted alphabetically. The alphabetical guest list provides the room numbers and the letters are then placed in the appropriate pigeonholes in the letter rack. Large envelopes, packages, and registered letters are stored in a separate place. A notification memo is placed in the pigeonhole in the letter rack, asking the guest to collect the registered letter or package, either at the reception desk or information desk.

Mail for Departed Guests

Many guests will leave a forwarding address, filling in a mail-forwarding form (fig. 6-1). These are kept on file for a specified length of time. Once the expiration date passes, the cards should be removed. Any mail arriving after that date, or if no forwarding address was left, is returned to the sender via the post office.

Mail for Future Guests

Mail for guests yet to arrive is sorted into alphabetical order and kept to one side. The advance reservation list is checked for the guest's arrival date, a note made in the hotel diary that mail is being held, and on the appropriate date it is placed in the letter rack.

Registered Mail (Incoming)

Registered mail has to be signed for by an authorized person and entered into a log book with date and time of arrival and receipt number. It is then placed under lock and key or in the safe. If it is for guests, a notification memo is placed in the letter rack asking them to collect. The log book is signed by them to indicate that they have taken delivery.

Mail for Staff

The bell captain or housekeeper usually distributes any mail that arrives for in-house staff.

```
┌─────────────────────────────────────────────────────┐
│                                                       │
│                 MAIL  FORWARDING  FORM                │
│          *  *  *  *  PEACOCK  LODGE  *  *  *  *        │
│              JAMESVILLE,  FLORIDA  34247              │
│                                                       │
├───────────────────────────────────────────────────────┤
│ Mr   Mrs   Miss   Ms                  Room Number      │
├───────────────────────────────────────────────────────┤
│ Forwarding Address                                     │
│                                                        │
│                                                        │
├───────────────────────────────────────────────────────┤
│ Expiration Date                                        │
├───────────────────────────────────────────────────────┤
│ I agree to reimburse the hotel for any expense incurred in forwarding mail: │
│ Signed:                            Date:               │
├─────────────────────┬──────────────────────┬─────┬────┤
│ Date of redirection │     Description      │  $  │    │
├─────────────────────┼──────────────────────┼─────┼────┤
│                     │                      │     │    │
├─────────────────────┼──────────────────────┼─────┼────┤
│                     │                      │     │    │
├─────────────────────┼──────────────────────┼─────┼────┤
│                     │                      │     │    │
├─────────────────────┼──────────────────────┼─────┼────┤
│                     │                      │     │    │
├─────────────────────┼──────────────────────┼─────┼────┤
│                     │                      │     │    │
├─────────────────────┼──────────────────────┼─────┼────┤
│                     │                      │     │    │
└─────────────────────┴──────────────────────┴─────┴────┘
```

6-1. Mail-forwarding form.

Procedure for Handling Cash or Checks in the Mail

Any cash, checks, or money orders that arrive in the mail should be prelisted with date of receipt, amount, and sender's name and address. It is then handed to the cashier, who will sign for receipt and process it through the appropriate accounting records.

OUTGOING MAIL

1. A deadline time should be set for outgoing mail if it is to be ready for mailing that day.
2. Regular collection of mail from the various departments should

be made throughout the day; this will ease the pressure and buildup of outgoing mail before the mailman is due.

3. All mail should be sorted and weighed to ensure the correct postage charge is affixed. Overseas mail should be kept separate, as the postal rates are different.

4. Any post office receipts for registered mail, parcels, or recorded delivery should be glued in a special book kept for that purpose.

5. All outgoing hotel business mail should be put through the postage meter showing the correct date. Or, if postage stamps are used, a postage book should be kept, showing the expenditure on stamps.

Registered Mail (Outgoing)

Registered mail has to be handed in to the post office which will issue an official receipt. Return receipts are requested at time of mailing. Registered mail, as well as express mail, should be entered into a log book and the receipt glued in for safe keeping.

Pre-Paid Business Reply Cards or Envelopes

These cards and envelopes are used for establishing goodwill, for advertising all activities that hotels engage in, and for soliciting business. The hotel as the sender pays the postage if the recipient sends back the card or envelope. A permit must be obtained from the post office, and mail must conform to certain standards. A permit account is opened at the post office, and a deposit paid in advance.

Bulk Mail

Special rates are available for bulk mail. A permit must be obtained from the post office, and the mail must be presorted according to the rules laid down by the postal service.

Proof of Postage

If proof of postage is required the post office will issue a receipt which must be kept safe in the folder for receipts.

Express Mail Services

The United States postal services and other, private organizations, such as Federal Express, Purolator, and UPS, offer express mail services for letters and packages, guaranteeing delivery within a certain period of time.

Information on Mailing

Publications are issued by the U.S. Postal Service giving full information on all their services. These can be obtained from the post office and should be kept handy for reference.

POSTAL EQUIPMENT AND MACHINES

Letter and Package Scales

If a letter contains more than one or two sheets of paper it should be weighed on a letter scale to ensure that the correct amount of postage is affixed. All parcels and large packages should be weighed on parcel scales.

Stamps

Stamps come in rolls or books and are easily lost if they are loose. They should be kept in a stamp folder with separate divisions for each denomination. Stamps should be kept in a safe place under lock and key, and a record kept of their usage.

Postage Meters

If the volume of mail is high, a postage meter can save time. This machine can be leased or purchased from suppliers licensed by the post office. An advance purchase of postage is made from the post office, and the amount entered on the machine. As stamp value is printed, the amount on the machine is reduced until it reaches zero. Then another advance payment has to be made at the post office. Metered post has to be faced, securely bundled, and if not collected, placed in a mail box for metered mail. Care must be taken to change the meter to the correct date each day and to follow postal regulations regarding collection of metered mail.

FILING AND INDEXING

Filing is a process of systematically classifying and storing records so that information can be produced without unreasonable delay. Indexing is the systematic arrangement of information in strict alphabetical order. Even in the day of the computerized office, there will always be paperwork that has to be filed.

The basic principles of a good filing system are as follows:

Compactness and accessibility. Filing cabinets should not take up too much space. They should be situated so that drawers open easily and files are accessible.

Simplicity and elasticity. A good filing system should be simple and easy to understand and operate. It should also be capable of expansion if necessary.

Safety and security. Records may have to be kept for reference over a long period of time and must be adequately protected. Security measures should be taken for the safe custody of confidential and important files. Cabinets should be locked, and the keys held by responsible officials.

Speed and efficiency. The proof of a good filing system lies in the ease with which records can be found. Speed is essential, as delays are time-wasting and irritating. Filing should be kept up-to-date. If a file is removed an "out" guide with the date and name of the person or department that has taken the file should be inserted in its place. The files should be cleaned out regularly, and outdated records removed and placed in "dead files."

Methods of Filing

Although there is a method of flat filing, with documents placed one on top of the other in shallow drawers or box files, most businesses use some kind of vertical filing (fig. 6-2). The drawers in these files are fitted with rails for suspension files. Dividers in drawers are called "guides." A primary "guide" will show the main division and a "special

6-2. Vertical suspension filing (Courtesy of Roneo Ltd.).

guide" will indicate a special section of the files. There are several designs to choose from.

Classification

There are five basic classifications for filing: alphabetical, numerical, geographical, chronological (date order), and by subject matter. The basis of all these systems is the alphabetical filing of names of people, places, things, or subject matter. Even when the system is numerical, it requires an alphabetical cross-index.

> **Alphabetical.** Records are filed according to the first letter of the surname and then in order of the first letter of the first name. Surnames beginning with "Mac" or "Mc" are treated as though all begin with "Mac." The next letter in the name

determines the filing position. For example, McAlpine comes before MacArthur which comes before MacDonald. The "Mac" prefix is usually positioned at the beginning of the "M" filing. The same principle applies when the prefix is "Saint" or "St." Hyphenated names, such as Wynne-Jones, should be filed under the first surname, in this case "W," but a name such as S. Gabriel Brown is filed under "B." Titles should be disregarded.

Numerical. Documents or files are given numbers and filed in number order. This system is used in conjunction with an alphabetical index. To locate a particular file, it is necessary to consult the index first for the file number. Copies of bills or invoices are usually filed in numerical order.

Geographical. The location or address is used as the identifying heading. The arrangement would be by state, county, town, and street, then number or zip code. Within each geographical group, the alphabetical order is used.

Subject matter. All documents relating to a given subject are filed under one heading. For example, under "personnel," contracts, employment applications, and training programs, would be filed.

Chronological. Subject matter is filed in date order.

Indexing

The purpose of an index is to make it easy to locate any record in the system. Indexing can take any of the following forms:

A page. As in the index page at the back of a book.

Vertical. Cards arranged in drawers or trays.

Wheel index. Cards arranged around the circumference of a wheel as in figure 6-3. Hundreds of cards can be attached to one wheel, making this a suitable and speedy system for a large volume of records.

STATIONERY

The headings and color of stationery is a management decision and is chosen with care, as it forms part of the advertising and marketing program for the establishment. Paper sizes are standardized; those most commonly used are:

6-3.   Two-tier Rondofile (Courtesy of Myers & Son Ltd.).

Standard—8 1/2" x 11"
Legal—8 1/2" x 14"

Stationery should be kept stacked and clearly labeled in a clean dry cupboard, centrally situated. Colored cards should be inserted at the appropriate place as reminders that it is time to reorder.

Continuous Stationery

Bills, invoices, office forms, and memos can be ordered in continuous strips. These are separated by perforations so that the forms can be detached. Several copies of each form are produced by using "no carboned required" (NCR) paper.

THE COMPUTERIZED OFFICE

Microcomputer and software manufacturers are revolutionizing office procedures by introducing advanced technology and producing software systems for every office situation. Some of the equipment now found in many offices includes the following:

Electronic typewriters and video typewriters. Memory-writers with disk storage, screen display, automatic typing features, spell-check dictionaries, and many other features now allow the writer to perform a multiplicity of tasks, including: storing documents onto disks; making corrections quickly; moving, copying, or deleting blocks of text; automatically replacing a word, phrase, or sentence; paginating documents; printing out perfect letters and documents.

Word processors. Word-processing programs turn the computer into a word processor. With them the user can create, edit, insert, delete, replace, and move text readily. Information from data files can be integrated into basic documents. Frequently used forms, letters, contracts, and other documents are stored in files and can be readily individualized and copied.

Dot matrix printers. Charts, diagrams, patterns, and other artwork can be interfaced with text.

Daisywheel printer. Daisywheel printers can print text and graphics from a library of different types and styles.

Electronic laser printers. Sophisticated high speed electronic laser printing systems can produce computer generated forms, graphics, and text in various types, sizes, and styles at a rate of up to 120 impressions per minute.

Copiers

Almost every office includes some kind of photocopying machines. The more sophisticated machines can reproduce and collate complicated copy in many ways. For example, the Xerox 1050 Marathon copier shown in figure 6-4 has, in addition to the basics, the following features:

- Operating speed of 55 copies per minute
- Automatic computer forms feeder (CFF) that accepts up to 300 sheets of unburst fan-fold paper
- CFF selective copying whereby only selected pages are copied
- Deletion control allowing user to delete lines or paragraphs during copying

Among other equipment now found in the office of many hotels are the following. While front desk personnel may never have occasion to operate these machines, they should know of their existence and purposes.

Labeling systems. The system automatically labels or addresses light to midweight material.

Folder inserter. Inserts documents into envelopes and seals them.

6-4. 1050 Marathon copier (Courtesy of Xerox Corporation).

It interfaces with most postage meters via a postage meter conveyor.

List management system. A floppy disk stores lists of the names and addresses for mailing lists, providing automatic label and report generation.

Addresser. Automatically cuts and applies liquid- or heat-activated labels to documents or envelopes.

Binder. Precut strips give multipage reports professional binding.

CONTROL SYSTEMS

In the hotel and catering industry, as in all other types of business, there are monitoring systems known as controls. These keep track of monies and inventories, promoting efficiency and reducing the chance of pilferage.

Bar/Restaurant Control System
(With Permission of NCR)

The bar/restaurant control system allows cashiers in the hotel's bar and restaurant to post charges directly to a guest's folios. One system manufactured by NCR (fig. 6-5), for example, has the following functions:

Room status inquiry. Verifies the occupancy of a room in the hotel and provides the occupant's name

Pre-inquiry. Verifies guest status before entry of charge sales data

Room charge. Adds the bar or restaurant charges to the hotel guest's folio

Account inquiry. Verifies a guest's credit account status before entry of charge sales data

Account charge. Updates a charge account with new charges

6–5. A computerized bar/restaurant control system (Courtesy of NCR Corporation).

Void transaction. Voids a room charge or account charge
Reentry transaction. Reenters data if MLS is offline

Audit Roll Control

Checks should be made that the totals registered on the tally rolls
of the tills in bars and restaurants agree with the cash returned by the
cashiers. A supervisor should clear the machines and reset them to zero
at various times during the day.

Inventory Control

It is essential that control should be kept over all inventory, be it
food, liquor, or items of equipment as shortages or overstock can be
costly. A good system for monitoring, ordering, and recording items
will prevent problems. The basis of a good inventory control system
includes the following:

1. When merchandise is received into the kitchen, cellar, linen
   closet, or other sections, it should be checked against the delivery ticket and copy of the order, and then entered into a mer-
   chandise-received book.
2. Merchandise is shelved and entered onto the inventory record
   card for each item (fig. 6-6).
3. Departmental requisition slips are used for booking items out
   of the stores, cellars, linen closet, and so on (fig. 6-7).
4. These requisiton slips are also used to record the items booked
   out on the inventory cards.
5. Requisition slips are also used to compile an issues analysis
   report for management showing the movement of stock.
6. Regular physical inventory counts should be made to ensure
   that the balance in stock agrees with the balance on the inventory record card.

If a computerized inventory control system is used, the trafficking
of merchandise will be posted to the records automatically by the computer, but a physical inventory check should still be done periodically.

Item				Suppliers:		
Description						
Date	Quantity	Details	Unit Value $	Received In $	Booked Out $	Stock In Hand $

6-6. Inventory record card.

PAYROLL

There are many patented payroll systems especially adapted to meet the requirements of individual employers. Computerized systems are programed to provide the same information and records. The basic principles and requirements underlying all systems are the same.

1. To provide descriptive information about each employee, such as name, social security number, marital status, exemption codes, and pay rate.
2. To keep a record of hours worked.

			No.	
		REQUISITION		

To

From

Quantity	Unit	Details	Unit Value	$

Received by   Authorized by

6-7. Requisition form.

3. To calculate gross earnings and keep a record of the cumulative earnings of each employee.
4. To calculate the net earnings after deduction of federal and state taxes, and other voluntary deductions.
5. To keep a record of cumulative taxes withheld.
6. To keep a record of any voluntary deductions withheld.
7. To provide a record of the cumulative Federal Unemployment Compensation Tax (FUTA) and Federal Insurance Contributions Act Tax (FICA).
8. To prepare payroll, payslips, and paychecks for employees.

The Department of Treasury
Internal Revenue Service (IRS)

An Employers' Tax Guide, which lists their tax responsibilities, is issued to all employers. It details requirements for withholding, depositing, reporting, and paying taxes. Withholding tables show the amounts of federal and state taxes that must be withheld from employees.

In general taxes are withheld from the employees' taxable earnings based on their wages and number of withholding allowances claimed. A Wages and Tax Statement (W-2 Form) must be furnished by the employer to the employee showing the gross earnings for the calendar year and withholdings for FICA and income taxes.

Taxable Tips

Tips an employee receives are generally subject to withholding. Cash tips must be reported on Form 4070 to the employers by the tenth of the month after the tips are received. No report is required for months when tips are less than twenty dollars.

Recordkeeping

All records of employment tax must be kept by employers for four years and should be available for IRS review. Records should include:

1. Employee's identification number.
2. Amounts and dates of all wages, annuity, and pension payments.
3. Amounts of tips reported.
4. The fair-market value of "in-kind" wages paid.
5. Names, addresses, social security numbers, and occupations of employees and independent contractors.
6. Dates of employees and recipients employment.
7. Periods for which employees and independent contractors were paid while absent due to sickness or injury, and the amount and weekly rate of payments you or third-party payers made to them.
8. Copies of employees' and independent contractors' income tax withholding allowance certificates.
9. Dates and amounts of tax deposit employers made.
10. Copies of returns filed.
11. Records of allocated tips.
12. Records of fringe benefits provided, including substantiation required under code section 274 and related regulations.

A calendar in the Employer's Guide issued by the Department of Labor quotes all the form numbers and gives important dates when the tax returns have to be filed.

CHAPTER SUMMARY

This chapter summarizes all the tasks front office personnel may have to carry out in addition to front desk reception work. Not all hotels/motels have specialized staff whose jobs are confined to one particular area; therefore, a sound knowledge of general business practice is always useful.

Important points discussed are:

- Handling incoming and outgoing mail
- A well-constructed business letter
- Procedures for handling cash or checks through the mail
- Postage meters
- Correct methods of filing and indexing
- Equipment in a computerized office
- Control systems
- Payroll
- IRS records

FOR DISCUSSION

1. The front desk usually has periods of high and low activity during the day. Discuss the tasks that could be dealt with by front office personnel during the low-activity periods.
2. You work in the front office of a medium-size resort hotel, and your manager has given you the responsibility of replying to routine letters and inquiries by mail. Discuss what you consider good and bad examples of a business letter.
3. Nothing is more irritating than being told to wait while someone goes through an inefficient filing system trying to locate a document or information. Discuss the importance of a good filing and indexing system from the point of view of business efficiency.
4. Gather information and discuss the developments and features of the latest office equipment on the market.
5. Discuss the types of control systems that are incorporated into the latest computerized hotel-management systems.
6. Discuss the importance of keeping accurate payroll records, from the point of view of the employee and the employer.

KEY TERMS

Registered mail
Bulk mail
Filing and indexing
Video typewriters
Word processors
Electronic laser printers
Dot matrix printers
Daisywheel printers
Copiers
Bar/restaurant control systems
Audit roll controls
Inventory controls

CHAPTER QUIZ

1. In addition to reception and reservation duties, what other tasks should front office personnel be able to perform competently?

2. What are the desirable features of a good business letter and what rules should be followed when drafting a letter?

3. Explain briefly how you would deal with:
   a. Mail for guests in residence
   b. Mail for departed guests
   c. Mail for guests yet to arrive
   d. Registered letters
   e. Cash, checks, or money orders arriving by mail
   f. Outgoing mail

4. What are the basic principles of a good filing system?

5. Describe different methods of filing and give the five basic classifications for filing.

6. File the following names in the correct order:
   Mr. J. St. Ives
   Mr. R. Macdonald

Miss A. Porter Smith
Captain L. Wynne-Hulme
Mrs. Cynthia Smythe
Miss Louella Smythe
Miss Abegail Smythe
Mr. S. Ortego
Ms. B. Martinelli
Mr. K. Dietkop
Ms. M. Ramos

7. Describe some of the latest equipment and machines found in a modern computerized office.

8. What are the features of a word processor?

9. Describe some of the functions a modern midvolume copier can perform.

10. Describe some of the capabilities of a computerized bar/restaurant control system.

11. What is the basis of a good inventory control system?

12. What are the basic principles and requirements of any payroll system?

13. What records must be kept for IRS review and for how long?

7

REPORTS AND
STATISTICS

In modern business organizations, reports, statistics, graphics, and charts are prepared as aids and tools of management. They provide information that helps guide and control the affairs of the business and assists executives in making decisions on policy and future developments. Percentages, ratios, and averages are helpful in presenting the operational information in a simple manner.

It is an embarrassing situation if one cannot calculate a simple percentage, ratio, or average without the aid of a calculator, so staff should have an understanding of basic arithmetical calculation.

PERCENTAGES

The simple method of calculating percentages is as follows: Multiply quantity by rate and move decimal point two places to left.

Example 1:
What is 6.5% of $32.40?

(rate) (quantity)
$32.40 \times 6.5 = 210.60$. Move decimal point 2 places to left
= $2.106 (round up to $2.11)

Example 2:
What percentage is $525 of $1750?

> 52500   add 2 zeros to the top figure
> ÷ 1750   and divide by the bottom figure
> = 30%

Example 3:
What percentage of $3.50 is 77 cents?

> 7700
> ÷ 350
> = 22%

ACCOUNTING RATIOS

A ratio is a way of expressing the relationship of one figure to another, for example:

$$\frac{\$75,000}{\$300,000} = \text{a ratio of 1:4 (\$75,000 goes into \$300,000 4 times)}$$

Expressed as a percentage

$$\frac{\$75,000 \times 100}{\$300,000} = 25\%$$

$$\frac{\$60,000}{\$15,000} = \text{a ratio of 4:1}$$

Expressed as a percentage

$$\frac{\$60,000 \times 100}{\$15,000} = 400\%$$

AVERAGES

When preparing statistics on guest spending power, length of stay, and room sales it is common practice to use averages (fig. 7-1). There are three methods of arriving at averages:

Mean. Add weekly totals and divide by the number of weeks they
cover.
Median. Arrange the figures in either ascending or descending
order. If the number is odd, select the middle figure. If the

MEAN		MEDIAN $	MODE $
Week No.	Room Sales $		
1	3680	3920	3680
2	3760	3840	3760*
3	3720	3760	3720
4	3760	3760	3760*
		—— median	
5	3680	3760	3680
6	3760	3720	3760*
7	3840	3680	3840
8	3920	3680	3920
Total	8)30120		
Average	3765	3760	3760

*3760 is the mode in this scale.

7-1. Averages.

number is even, add the two middle figures together and divide by two.

Mode. The most frequently repeated figure in the series.

The Moving Average

This method of calculating an average is favored by the hotel industry. It can show a trend over a period of time and eliminates the effects of seasonal fluctuations. Sales figures are listed by month. At the end of each month the top figure is removed and the latest month's figure is added. A new average is calculated. Averages can be based on three months, as in the example below, or more.

Month	*Sales*
January	$ 5,750
February	5,500
March	6,300
Total	$ 17,550 (divided by 3 = $5,850 average)
February	5,500
March	6,300
April	6,700
Total	$ 18,500 (divided by 3 = $6,167 average)

SALES-MIX PERCENTAGES

The term *sales mix* refers to the composition of the total volume of sales and the percentage of that total contributed by each part.

Revenue Source	Sales	% of Sales Total
Room sales	$ 130,000	52%
Restaurant sales	80,000	32
Bar sales	35,000	14
Other	5,000	2
Total	$ 250,000	100%

The method of calculation is as follows

Room sales

$$\frac{130,000 \times 100}{250,000} = 52\%$$

Restaurant sales

$$\frac{80,000 \times 100}{250,000} = 32\%$$

Bar sales

$$\frac{35,000 \times 100}{250,000} = 14\%$$

Other

$$\frac{5,000 \times 100}{250,000} = 2\%$$

ROOM/BED OCCUPANCY

The sale of accommodation produces the highest percentage of the total revenue of most hotels. Daily occupancy reports are prepared and analyzed. From them management can determine whether the hotel is operating to its maximum efficiency.

Room Occupancy

To calculate the room occupancy percentage, multiply the number of occupied rooms by one hundred and divide by the number of rooms available for rental. For the percentage to be accurate, the number of OOO rooms (out of order) must first be deducted from the total salable room inventory in the hotel.

Total number of salable rooms in hotel	200
Less number of OOO rooms	-18
Equals number of rooms available for rental	182
Number of rooms occupied	135

$$\text{Room occupancy percentage} = \frac{135 \times 100}{182} = 74.2\%$$

Bed Occupancy

Another important statistic is to calculate the actual bed (sleeper) occupancy percentage, or the number of guests staying at the hotel. The equation is similar to that for room occupancy. Multiply the number of sleepers by one hundred and divide by the maximum number of guests (subtracting beds in OOO rooms).

Number of sleepers = 245
Maximum guest capacity = 324

$$\text{Bed occupancy percentage} = \frac{245 \times 100}{324} = 75.7\%$$

Average Daily Rate

The average daily room rate can also be calculated as follows:

Day's revenue from sale of rooms	$13,003.90
Divided by the number of salable rooms	÷ 182
Equals the average daily rate	$71.45

AVERAGE LENGTH OF STAY

To assist the management in organizing staff work schedules and rosters to make the most efficient use of staff and equipment, it is helpful to calculate the average length of stay of the guest. For example, during the course of one week four hundred guests were booked into a hotel. To calculate the average length of stay an average week is taken during the high season and low season. The number of guests is multiplied by their length of stay (e.g., 80 guests stay 3 nights = 240 sleeper nights). The total sleeper nights for the week is divided by the number of guests to get the average length of stay (fig. 7-2).

The Department of Commerce, Division of Tourism, publishes such statistics as guidelines for the hotel industry. For example, according to a Florida survey,

Length of Stay	Air Visitors	Auto Visitors
Short Stays	*Annual %*	*Annual %*
1 Night	7.5	3.0
2 Nights	8.6	6.9
3 Nights	10.1	10.6
4 Nights	11.1	10.6
5 Nights	9.1	9.4
6 Nights	6.5	7.3
Total %	53.3	47.8
Possible Long Weekends		
3 Nights	10.1	10.6
4 Nights	11.1	10.6
5 Nights	9.5	9.4
Total %	30.7	30.6

INTERNATIONAL VISITORS

Many hotels maintain records and statistics relating to international visitors and their nationality. Tourists from other countries account for a great deal of revenue to some large hotels; a watchful eye is kept on these percentages so that advertising campaigns can be planned to attract foreign visitors. Data on international travel are made available by the United States Department of Transportation and International Air Travel Statistics. In 1984, for example, of the 9 million or so visitors to the United States, over 3 million came from Europe, and over 700,000 from South America.

Length of Stay	Number of Guests	Sleeper Nights
1 night ×	102 =	102
2 nights ×	130 =	260
3 nights ×	80 =	240
4 nights ×	40 =	160
5 nights ×	28 =	140
6 nights ×	10 =	60
7 nights ×	10 =	70
Total	400 =	1032

Average length of stay = $\frac{1032}{400}$ = 2.58 nights

7-2. Average length of stay.

Percentage of Foreign Visitors

A hotel's records showed the following figures

Total number of international visitors	2,850 x 100
Divided by total number of guests	÷ 10,200
Equals percentage of foreign visitors	27.9%

Country of Origin	Number	%
Great Britain	912	32
Europe	1,140	40
Scandinavia	342	12
South America	285	10
Others	171	6
Total	2,850	100

HOUSEKEEPER'S REPORT

In some hotels the head housekeeper has to prepare a room-occupancy report (fig. 7-3), from which the number of occupied rooms, OOO rooms, and vacant rooms are calculated.

Date: 1 June						Time: 2200 hrs	
Floor 1		Floor 2		Floor 3		Floor 4	
101	✓	201	✓	301	OOO	401	vacant
102	✓	202	✓	302	✓	402	OOO
103	✓	203	✓	303	✓	403	✓
104	✓	204	✓	304	vacant	404	✓
105	OOO	205	vacant	305	vacant	405	✓
106	✓	206	vacant	306	vacant	406	OOO
107	✓	207	✓	307	✓	407	vacant
108	✓	208	✓	308	✓	408	✓
109	✓	209	OOO	309	✓	409	OOO
110	✓	210	vacant	310	vacant	410	vacant
	9		6		5		4

✓ Occupied	Maximum No. of Rooms for Let	32
OOO Out of Order	Rooms Out of Order	6

ANALYSIS:

Room Occupancy % = $\dfrac{\text{No. of Rooms Let}}{\text{Maximum No. of Rooms for Let}} = \dfrac{24}{40} \times \dfrac{100}{1} = 60\%$

Out of Order % = $\dfrac{\text{Rooms OOO}}{\text{Maximum No. of Rooms for Let}} = \dfrac{6}{40} \times \dfrac{100}{1} = 15\%$

Rooms Vacant % = $\dfrac{\text{Rooms Unoccupied}}{\text{Maximum No. of Rooms for Let}} = \dfrac{10}{40} \times \dfrac{100}{1} = 25\%$

(Signature) HEAD HOUSEKEEPER

NOTE: √ = occupied

7-3. Housekeeper's room occupancy report.

GRAPHS AND CHARTS

Many hotels maintain wall graphs and charts that are used to gain an overall picture of hotel occupancy without having to refer to detailed records. The information tabulated below is shown in figure 7-4 as a graph and figure 7-5 as a bar chart.

Date	Room Occupancy	Bed Occupancy
May 15	60%	60%
June 15	64	65
July 15	80	83
August 15	99	97
September 15	85	84

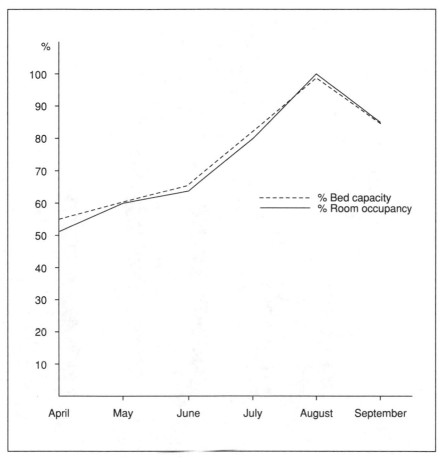

7-4. A comparative room occupancy/bed occupancy shown in graph form.

FORECASTING

Occupancy forecasts are very useful tools of management: sales revenue can be projected and results measured later against the forecast; management can plan projects such as hotel maintenance and remodeling for low-occupancy periods; advertising campaigns can be planned to improve low-occupancy percentages; heads of departments can forecast their purchase requirements and plan labor and vacation rosters.

Many hotels have computers that produce forecast printouts of future room and guest occupancy. Front office reservations personnel should still be able to project an accurate forecast without the help of a computer.

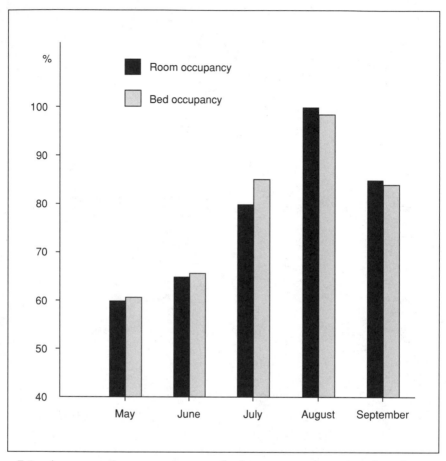

7-5. A comparative room occupancy/bed occupancy shown as a bar chart.

The forecast can cover any period of time. This depends entirely on management policy. The information necessary to project a forecast includes the following:

1. The actual number of rooms confirmed as shown on the reservations chart or scan.
2. A study of the reservations chart for the same period last year.
3. A calculation of average number of walk-in guests.
4. A calculation of the percentage of no-shows.
5. A note of any changes between last year and now that are likely to affect the forecast.
6. A basic formula for the calculation of guest occupancy.

$$\frac{\text{Actual number of guests for the period} = 415}{\text{Number of rooms available for rental} = 297} = 1.40 \text{ guests per room}$$

Using the formula, follow the forecast chart in figure 7-6 that covers the period from Wednesday, 3 October, to Saturday, 13 October (11 days). The percentage calculations follow:

Wednesday	Forecast Rooms		%Occupancy
10/3	$\frac{180 \times 100}{297}$	=	60.6
Totals (11 days × 297)	$\frac{2487 \times 100}{3267}$	=	76.1

CHAPTER SUMMARY

This chapter emphasizes the importance of reports and statistics as aids and tools of management. Statistics can be presented in many ways: percentages, ratios, or averages, shown in numerical or graph charts. Statistics are used to set targets and goals for management and employees.

Important points or topics discussed:

- How to calculate simple percentages, ratios, and averages without the aid of a calculator
- The meaning of the term *sales mix*
- The importance of room/bed occupancy percentages
- How to calculate the average length of stay of a guest
- International visitors
- Forecasting

FOR DISCUSSION

1. Why are reports and statistics essential to management and what type of information do they provide that helps guide and control management decisions?
2. Discuss the importance of the sales mix percentages. What information do these percentages provide to management?

* * * * PEACOCK LODGE * * * *

Jamesville, Florida 34567

Max: Rooms 297
Max: Guests 415

3-13 October
11-day forecast

Date	ACTUAL Rooms Reserved	FORECAST Rooms	Guests	Arrivals	Departures	% Occupancy
Wednesday 10/3	175	180	252	101	88	60.6
Thursday 10/4	151	170	238	100	110	57.2
Friday 10/5	297	297	415	251	124	100.0
Saturday 10/6	287	297	415	74	74	100.0
Sunday 10/7	68	77	108	50	270	25.9
Monday 10/8	75	108	151	91	60	36.4
Tuesday 10/9	204	242	339	200	66	81.5
Wednesday 10/10	297	297	415	146	91	100.0
Thursday 10/11	297	297	415	139	139	100.0
Friday 10/12	238	297	415	168	168	100.0
Saturday 10/13	154	225	315	71	143	75.8
Totals	2,243	2,487	3,478	1,391	1,333	76.1

LAST WEEK'S SUMMARY

Date	Rooms (Forecast)	Rooms (Actual)	% Occupancy (Forecast)	% Occupancy (Actual)
Wednesday 9/26	195	199	65.7	67.0
Thursday 9/27	235	258	79.1	86.9
Friday 9/28	193	200	65.0	67.3
Saturday 9/29	194	184	65.3	62.0
Sunday 9/30	119	106	40.1	35.7
Monday 10/1	158	164	53.2	55.2
Tuesday 10/2	154	167	51.9	56.2
Totals	1,248	1,278	60.0	61.5

7-6. A forecast sheet.

168

3. "A bed unoccupied is revenue lost." Discuss the importance of room and bed occupancy figures.
4. From the point of view of staff organization, discuss why the average length of stay of the guest is an important statistic.
5. Why is forecasting future occupancy essential from the point of view of staff organization?

KEY TERMS

Accounting ratios
Averages
Moving average
Sales mix
Room/bed occupancy
Average length of stay
Forecasting

CHAPTER QUIZ

1. Calculate the following percentages (without calculator).
    a. 7.5% of $22
    b. 17.5% of $108
    c. 12% of $22,360
    d. 15% of $42,320
    e. 22% of $104,500

2. Calculate the following percentages (without calculator).
    a. $15,600 of $120,000
    b. 780 of 1200
    c. 1428 of 2100
    d. 32 of 480
    e. 108 of 720

3. Calculate the following ratios.
    a. $\dfrac{\$22,000}{\$110,000}$

    b. $\dfrac{\$35,000}{\$7,500}$

4. Complete the following table.

	Vernon Hotel	
Length of Stay	*Number of Guests*	*Sleeper Nights*
1 night	180	
2 nights	120	
3 nights	140	
4 nights	80	
5 nights	160	
6 nights	30	
7 nights	50	
Total		
Average length of stay		

5. Complete the following table.

	Mean		
Week No.	*Room Sales*	*Median*	*Mode*
	$		
1	2860		
2	2740		
3	2730		
4	2770		
5	2950		
6	2870		
7	2790		
8	2780		
9	2790		
Average			

6. From the following information calculate the room occupancy percentage.

Total number of rooms in hotel = 88
Number of rooms out of order = 6
Number of rooms occupied = 59

7. Complete the following table.

Sales Mix	$	%
Accommodation sales	172,800	
Restaurant sales	96,000	
Bar sales	41,600	
Other sales	9,600	
Total sales		

8. Complete the following table.

Atlanta Hotel		
Number of Rooms: 300		Guest Capacity: 520

Date	Rooms Occupied	Rate of Room Occupancy
1986		
June 20	216	
July 20	264	
August 20	285	
September 20	279	
October 20	243	
November 20	219	

9. Complete the following equation and table.

$$\frac{\text{Total number of overseas visitors}}{\text{Total number of visitors}} = \frac{3152}{9850} = \quad \%$$

Overseas Visitors	Number	%
French	598	
German	536	
Japanese	347	
Scandinavian	284	
Great Britain	473	

10.   Complete the following table.

| | Peacock Lodge | | | | |
Week Ending	Anchor Bar $	Tartan Bar $	Restaurant $	Coffee Shop $	Total $
7/4	1240.20	1232.10	2275.60	1250.30	
7/11	1243.40	1225.10	2282.40	1233.10	
7/18	1226.40	1220.20	2296.40	1242.10	
7/25	1236.40	1226.40	2302.60	1226.00	
Total					
8/1	1248.60	1236.10	2277.30	1246.20	
8/8	1252.50	1232.20	2250.40	1238.20	
8/15	1234.40	1244.10	2256.20	1224.10	
8/22	1244.20	1228.20	2278.60	2236.80	
8/29	1258.40	1236.10	2246.20	1232.30	
Total					
9/5	1232.70	1222.30	2266.80	1240.50	
9/12	1220.80	1230.10	2287.60	1231.20	
9/19	1242.60	1240.00	2252.40	1239.30	
9/26	1244.00	1243.10	2268.40	1227.10	
Total					
Totals					

11.   Based on the table in question 10, answer the following questions.
   a. What percent of the total revenue for the period are the total revenues for each of the following?
      (1) Anchor bar
      (2) Tartan bar
      (3) Restaurant
      (4) Coffee shop
   b. Calculate the average revenue per week for the restaurant over the period.

    c. If during the period the restaurant paid out $10,339.32 for food and supplies, calculate:
      (1) The gross profit in monetary terms
      (2) The gross profit as a percent of revenue

    d. What is the average spent per customer in the coffee shop if 4,723 customers were served?

    e. What percent of the total revenue for August was the revenue from the Tartan bar?

12. You are asked to project an eleven-day room occupancy forecast for your hotel: What information would you need?

13. Discuss forecasts as a tool and aid for management, their uses and advantages.

8

LEGAL ASPECTS

The specifics of the laws governing the hotel and tourism industry are complex, and rules and regulations may vary from state to state. Therefore, it is only possible to deal very briefly with the basic underlying principles of the laws as they relate to the work of front office personnel.

Copies of the rules, from which much of this chapter was taken, can be obtained from the Department of Business Regulation, Division of Hotels and Restaurants, located in most state capitals.

DEFINITIONS (AS USED IN THIS CHAPTER)

"'Division'. means Department of Business Regulations, Division of Hotels and Restaurants.

'Operator'. means owner, operator, keeper, proprietor, lessee, manager, assistant manager, employee, desk clerk, agent or employee of a public lodging establishment.

'Guest'. means any guest, tenant, lodger, boarder, or occupant of a public lodging establishment.

'Public lodging establishment'. means any building or group of buildings within a single complex of buildings which is kept, used, maintained or advertised as, or held out to the public to be a place where sleeping or housekeeping accommodations are supplied for payment to transient or permanent guests or tenants.

'Single complex buildings'. means all buildings which are owned, managed, controlled and operated under one business name, have a common street address, and are situated on the same tract of land which is not separated by a public street or highway.

'Transient occupancy'. means occupancy when it is the intention of the parties that the occupancy will be temporary."

GENERAL RULES

"The 'Division' is responsible for carrying out the laws relating to the inspection or regulations of public lodging establishments, for the purpose of safeguarding the public health, safety and welfare. The 'Division' is also responsible for ascertaining that no establishment licensed by it engages in any misleading or unethical practices.

"The 'Division' shall inspect each public lodging establishment a certain number of times annually and for this purpose the 'Division' or its contractual designee shall have the right of entry and access to the establishment at any reasonable time. Public lodging establishments are required to obtain a license which must be displayed in a prominent place and renewed annually. This license and renewal thereof will only

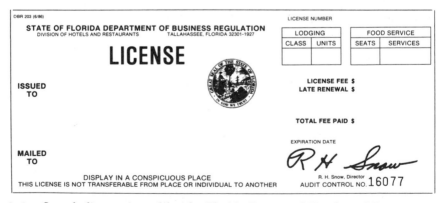

8–1. Sample license issued by the Florida Bureau of Hotels and Restaurants Licensing department (Courtesy of the Department of Business Regulations, Division of Hotels and Restaurants, Florida).

CITY OF SARASOTA
1984-1985 OCCUPATIONAL LICENSE

Amount

License Number

854226

Dated   For Period Commencing   and Ending

September 30th, 1985

IN CONSIDERATION OF THE AMOUNT SHOWN HEREIN PAID TO THE FINANCE DIRECTOR OF THE CITY OF SARASOTA, FLORIDA
THE NAMED PERSON, FIRM OR CORPORATION IS LICENSED TO ENGAGE IN BUSINESS.

Business Name and Mailing Address

Name and Address of Business

Owner/Manager Name

This license does not permit the holder to operate in violation of any City Law or Ordinance.
Any change in location or ownership must be approved by City License Department.

Classification	Description	License Tax	Penalty	Total Tax

TOTAL RECEIVED

JOHN T. HAYLETT
Finance Director

By _____

Post This License in a Conspicuous Place at your Business Location.

8–2. Occupational license (Courtesy of the City of Sarasota's Licensing department).

be issued to establishments operated, managed or controlled by a person of good moral character."

GENERAL REQUIREMENTS

"It is a general requirement that:

1. Roofs, walls, ceilings, floors, steps, windows, transoms, shelves, fixtures etc. shall be kept in good repair, cleaned and painted where applicable.
2. Attics, basements, boilerrooms and storage rooms shall be kept free of debris and flammables.
3. Insects, vermin, rodents, termites etc. shall be exterminated.

4. Outside garbage receptacles must be kept covered with a tight cover at all times.
5. The yards and alleys of the premises shall be kept clean and free of debris.
6. Employees quarters and furnishings will be kept clean and in good condition."

SAFETY REQUIREMENTS

The State Fire Marshall rules specify the general requirements and standards to be adhered to by public lodging establishments and copies of these rules, which set out the regulations in detail, can be obtained from the division. Basically the requirements state:

"a. The number of fire extinguishers required for each floor, for Class A fires, ordinary combustibles, and the maximum travel distance to the nearest fire extinguisher.
b. Fire extinguishers required for Class B fires, flammable liquids, grease and oil, etc.
c. Fire extinguishers required for Class C fires—electrical.
d. Compulsory regulations now exist for all public lodging establishments to be equipped with sprinkler systems and smoke detector systems.
e. To prevent fire or injury, defective wiring shall be replaced and kept in good repair. No extension cords shall be used.
f. Halls, closets, stairways, entrances and exits shall be kept free from obstruction and fire hazards.
g. Halls must be kept clean, ventilated and well lighted day and night, and stair runners must be kept in good condition.
h. Hand rails shall be installed on all stairways and guard rails around all porches and steps.
i. There must be adequate means of exit from dining area and kitchen. All exit doors must swing outwards and be equipped with automatic self-closing hardware.
j. Exits shall be clearly marked with approved illuminated exit signs."

PUBLIC LODGING ESTABLISHMENTS' RIGHTS AS PRIVATE ENTERPRISES

"Public lodging establishments are private enterprises and the 'operator' has the right to refuse accommodations or service to any person who is objectionable or undesirable to the 'operator', but such refusal shall not be based upon race, creed, color or sex, physical disability or national origin."

REFUSAL OF ADMISSION AND EJECTION OF UNDESIRABLE GUESTS

"The 'operator' of any public lodging establishment may remove or cause to be removed:

a. any 'guest' or 'transient' guest who while on the premises is intoxicated, immoral, profane, lewd or brawling, or who indulges in any language or conduct which disturbs the peace or comfort of other guests, or which injures the reputation, dignity or standing of the establishment.

b. any guest who fails to make payment of rent at the agreed upon check-out time or in the case of a public food service establishment fails to make payment for food, beverages or service.

c. any person who in the opinion of the 'operator', the continued entertainment of who would be detrimental to the establishment.

"The admission to or removal from such establishment shall not be upon race, creed, color, sex or physical disability or national origin.

"The 'operator' shall notify either orally or in writing such guest that the establishment no longer desires to entertain him/her, and request that the guest shall depart immediately from the establishment. If the guest has made payment in advance at the time notice is given, such unused portion of the advance payment shall be tendered to the guest.

"Any guest who remains or attempts to remain after being requested to leave may be guilty of a misdemeanor. The 'operator' may call upon a law enforcement officer for assistance to remove any person found illegally on the premises."

THE GUEST REGISTER

"It is the duty of the 'operator' to maintain at all times a register signed by or for the guests who occupy rental units within the establishment, showing the dates and rates charged for the occupation of the rental units. This register shall be available for inspection by the 'Division' at any time."

RULES OF THE ESTABLISHMENT

"Any 'operator' of a public lodging establishment may establish rules and regulations for the management of the establishment. These must be printed and posted in a prominent place.

"The rules and regulations control the responsibilities and obligations of all parties, and each guest or employee staying, sojourning, eating or employed in the establishment shall conform and abide by such rules and regulations as they are deemed to be a special contract between 'operator' and each guest or employee using the facilities of the public lodging establishment."

LAW OF CONTRACT

The specifics of contract law vary from state to state or country to country but according to most,

"A contract is an agreement enforceable by law between two or more parties. Though every contract is an agreement not every agreement is a contract. To be enforceable in law every contract must contain certain elements, absence of any of these elements renders the contract either void, voidable or unenforceable." The essential elements of a contract are:

"1. There must be an initial INTENTION by both parties to enter into a contract.
2. There must be an OFFER by one party and an unconditional ACCEPTANCE by the other party.
3. CONSIDERATION either in money, goods or services, must be promised or given in return for value offered.
4. There must be a genuine CONSENT by both parties.
5. There must be a POSSIBILITY of performance.
6. Each party must have the legal CAPACITY to contract."

BOOKING CONTRACTS

A booking contract between a guest and a public lodging establishment may come into being in several ways:

In writing
Telex

Telephone
Central reservations system
Travel agent
Walk-in

The express terms usually contained in a booking contract are those governing:

a. confirmation and method of payment
b. cancellation by either the guest or the establishment
c. any alteration to the terms by the establishment
d. liability by the establishment for guest's property
e. liability of the establishment for any unforeseen circumstances

A breach of contract occurs when one of the parties fails to perform any one of the terms of the contract.

ROOM RATES

"In each public lodging establishment renting by day or week, there shall be posted in a plainly legible manner and in a conspicuous place in each rental unit, the rates at which the unit is rented."

LIABILITY FOR PROPERTY OF GUESTS

"The 'operator' of a public lodging establishment is under no obligation to accept for safekeeping any monies, jewelry or precious stones belonging to any guest, and if any are accepted for safekeeping, he shall not be liable for loss thereof unless such loss was the proximate result of fault or negligence of the 'operator'.

"The liability of the 'operator' shall be limited for such loss if the public lodging establishment gives a receipt for the property, stating the value, on a form which states quite clearly that the liability for any such loss shall not exceed a stated amount.

"The 'operator' shall not be liable or responsible to any guest for the loss of wearing apparel, goods or other property except as provided in the previous paragraph, unless such loss occurred as the proximate result of fault or negligence of such 'operator'. The liability for such loss will be limited unless the guest has filed prior to the loss an inventory of the effects and value thereof."

UNCLAIMED PROPERTY

"Any property left in a public lodging establishment belonging to the guest who has left the premises with an outstanding account and without notice to the 'operator' shall become the property of the establishment after 90 days after written notice has been given to the guest by the 'operator'."

OBTAINING FOOD OR LODGINGS
WITH INTENT TO DEFRAUD

"Any person who obtains food, lodgings or other accommodations with an intent to defraud the 'operator' is guilty of a misdemeanor. If the value exceeds a certain sum, as set out in the rules, the guest may be guilty of a felony.

"Proof that lodgings or other accommodations were obtained by false pretense, by false or fictitious show of baggage or other property, by absconding without paying or offer of payment, or by surreptitiously removing or attempting to remove baggage shall constitute prima facie evidence of fraudulent intent. Any law enforcement officer or 'operator' who has probable cause to believe and does believe that a guest has obtained food and lodgings with intent to defraud, or that the person has illegally taken personal property belonging to the establishment from the premises, may take such a person into custody and detain him or her for such reasonable time as is necessary to take him/her before the nearest magistrate."

OVERBOOKINGS

Overbooking by a public lodging establishment licensed by the division is usually prohibited. Overbooking does occur and when an individual or party is deprived of accommodation or when such individual or party has prepaid reservations, in such cases the establishment is required to:

"a. make every effort to find comparable accommodation
b. on demand by the guest refund any monies deposited for such reservation, whether deposited with a travel agent, booking agent or the establishment.

"Violation of any provisions of this rule will subject the violator to disciplinary procedures as provided by the rules and regulations of the 'Division'."

UNETHICAL BUSINESS PRACTICE

"It is considered unethical business practice on the part of any public lodging establishment to impose an automatic charge apart from the room rate, for the provision or for the use of any of the conveniences contained in the room, but not limited to telephones. However, if such additional charges are disclosed to the guest at check-in time, or there is a statement on the guest registration card, or a clearly legible notice displayed on the check-in desk stating the additional or extra charges, then the imposition of such charges shall not be considered an unethical business practice."

FATALITIES

"Each establishment is required to file a report with the 'Division' if a fatality occurs in the establishment by other than natural causes. The report must contain the following information:

1. Name of the deceased.
2. Date of death.
3. Cause of death.
4. Name and address of the establishment."

AFTER HOURS DRINKING OF
LIQUOR ON LICENSED PREMISES

The law on after hours drinking of alcohol on licensed premises varies from state to state. In Florida, for example, all sales and consumption of liquor on any premises licensed by the state must cease at 2.30 a.m.

REVOCATION OR SUSPENSION OF LICENSES

It is not possible to go into all the regulations governing the revocation or suspension of licenses, fines, or procedures, but briefly they state (reproduced with permission of the Department of Business Regulation, Division of Hotels and Restaurants, Florida):

"The division may suspend or revoke the license of any public lodging establishment if the operator lets, leases or gives space for unlawful gambling purposes or where gambling is to be carried on in such establishment or in or upon any premises which are used in connection with, and are under the same charge, control, or management of such an establishment.

"The division may suspend or revoke the license of any public lodging establishment or public food service establishment when:

a. Any person interested in the operation of any such establishment within the preceding five years in this state, any other state, or the United States, has been adjudicated guilty of or forfeited a bond when charged with soliciting for prostitution, pandering, letting premises for prostitution, keeping a disorderly place, illegally dealing in narcotics, or any other crime reflecting on professional character.
b. Such establishment has been condemned by the local health authority for failure to meet sanitation standards or the premises has been condemned by the local authority because the premises are unsafe and unfit for human occupancy."

Copies of all the regulations governing hotels/motels and restaurants can be obtained from the Department of Business Regulation, Division of Hotels and Restaurants.

THE EQUAL EMPLOYMENT
OPPORTUNITY COMMISSION (EEOC)

The Equal Employment Opportunity Commission (EEOC) was created by Title VII of the Civil Rights Act of 1964. This law prohibits employment discrimination based on race, color, sex, religion, or national origin.

In 1978, the law was amended to include the Pregnancy Discrimination Act (PDA), which requires employers to treat pregnancy and pregnancy-related medical conditions as they do any other medical disability with respect to all terms and conditions of employment, including employee health benefits.

Since 1979, EEOC also has been responsible for enforcing other civil rights enactments: the Age Discrimination in Employment Act (ADEA), which protects workers between the ages of forty and seventy; the Equal Pay Act (EPA), which protects women and men performing substantially equal work against pay discrimination based on sex; and

Section 501 of the Rehabilitation Act of 1973, which prohibits discrimination against the handicapped.

Full detailed information of Title VII of the Civil Rights Act of 1964 and its amendments can be obtained from any area office of the EEOC.

THE FAIR LABOR STANDARDS ACT (FLSA)

The Fair Labor Standards Act of 1938 (FLSA), as amended, establishes standards for the minimum wage, overtime pay, recordkeeping, and child labor. It affects more than 50 million full- and part-time workers. Full information may be obtained from the U.S. Department of Labor, Employment and Standards Administration, Wage and Hours Division.

CHAPTER SUMMARY

This chapter deals briefly with the specifics of law.
Important points and topics discussed are:

- The general rules and requirements governing the running of a public lodging establishment
- Safety requirements
- The rights of the operator
- Undesirable guests
- The law of contract
- Booking contracts
- The liability of the hotel/motel for the property of guests
- Guests who obtain food and lodgings with an intent to defraud
- Overbooking
- Unethical business practice
- EEOC and FLSA

FOR DISCUSSION

1. Obtain from the Department of Business Regulation, Division of Hotels and Restaurants, a copy of the rules in your state and discuss the need for such rules to be understood if you are operating a public lodging establishment.
2. Discuss the importance of fire and safety regulations standards especially when running a public lodging establishment.

3. A hotel/motel operator is required by law to offer lodgings to bona fide travelers, but the management has certain rights when it comes to an "undesirable" guest. Discuss these rights.
4. Discuss how the law of contract applies to a reservation or booking at a hotel/motel.
5. Discuss the extent to which a hotel/motel operator is responsible for the property of a guest.
6. A hotel/motel operator is in the business of supplying food and accommodation to people in transit. Discuss the risks of fraud by guests who leave without settling their account. What precautions can the management take to reduce that risk?
7. Discuss what you understand by the term "unethical business practice."
8. The division has the authority to suspend or revoke the license of a public lodging establishment and to impose fines on the licensee. Discuss some of the reasons that can be given for the suspension or revocation of a license.
9. The after drinking hours regulations vary from state to state. Research and discuss the regulations as they apply in your state.
10. The U.S. Department of Labor issues a handy reference guide to the Fair Labor Standards Act. Research and discuss some of the important points such as:
    a. Basic wage standards
    b. Who is covered
    c. Tipped employees
    d. Employer-furnished facilities
    e. Subminimum wage provisions
    f. Recordkeeping
11. Discuss these terms used in the FLSA:
    a. Workweek
    b. Computing Overtime Pay
    c. Enforcement
    d. Recovery of Back Wage
    e. The Wage and Hour Division
    f. Equal Pay Provisions

KEY TERMS

Division
Operator
Transient occupancy

Class A, B, and C fires
Intention
Offer
Acceptance
Consideration
Consent
Possibility
Capacity
Unclaimed property
Intent to defraud
Overbooking
Unethical business practice
Equal Employment Opportunity Commission (EEOC)
Fair Labor Standards Act (FLSA)

CHAPTER QUIZ

1. Define the following terms as they relate to the Department of Business Regulation, Division of Hotels and Restaurants.
   a. Operator
   b. Public lodging establishment
   c. Division
   d. Transient occupancy
   e. Guest

2. What are the basic rules and regulations relating to the inspection and licensing of a public lodging establishment by the division?

3. Explain briefly the general fire safety regulations which relate to public lodging establishments.

4. Write briefly on a public lodging establishment's rights as a private enterprise. What rules govern the right of admission and ejection of undesirable guests?

5. Explain the basic elements required by the law of contract.

6. Write notes on the rules and regulations pertaining to:
   a. Guest registers
   b. Room rates
   c. Liability for the property of guests

      d. Unclaimed property

      e. Overbooking

      f. A fatality in the establishment

7. What would make you suspect that a guest had the intention of defrauding the establishment? What action would you take?

8. State what you understand by Title VII of the Civil Rights Act of 1964. Explain briefly the following:

      a. EEOC

      b. PDA

      c. ADEA

      d. EPA

      e. FLSA

9

ANCILLARY DUTIES, FIRST AID, SAFETY, AND SECURITY PRECAUTIONS

INTERDEPARTMENTAL COOPERATION

As the communications center of the establishment, the front office works closely with all other departments in the hotel. Only with such cooperation can the front office duties be carried out efficiently and effectively. Front office personnel must be aware, therefore, of the function and organization of all areas of work in the hotel, and the systems and methods used in each department.

The Housekeeping Department

One of the busiest executives in a hotel is the head housekeeper, who is responsible for the cleanliness and good order of all the rooms, bathrooms, hallways, public rooms, and offices. The Department of Business Regulation, Hotel and Restaurant Division sets out the standards of sanitation that must be adhered to by public lodging establish-ments.

Bed Occupancy and Room Availability Reports

It is the head housekeeper's responsibility to submit daily reports on room occupancy status to the front office, either via the computer system or whatever communication system is used in the establish-ment.

The Linen Room

The head housekeeper is responsible for the linen room, although in large hotels a separate linenkeeper is employed solely to maintain and care for all the sheets, pillowcases, towels and other linen which are used daily.

All linen should be kept in good repair and no soiled or torn linen must be issued. Inventory records must be maintained. When linen is sent to be laundered it is counted and checked, and when returned, it is again counted and checked. Generally speaking fresh linen is only issued on receipt of dirty linen. Any special requests such as extra pillows, blankets or cots in the rooms are referred to the head housekeeper. If such requests are made with room reservations, they are passed on to the housekeeping department through the internal communications system before the guest's arrival.

Restaurant linens are sometimes kept in a separate linen room, but the procedure is the same. The issue of clean table linen to the restaurant is usually on a requisition form. Staff must be made aware that the linen inventory is an asset of the business and costs money, therefore there must be no negligence in handling it.

Wake-up Calls and Room Service

Many guests ask for a wake-up call and use room service. Such requests are usually made to the switchboard operator or directly to room service. It is essential that careful note is made of the time of the wake-up call. All staff must make sure any requests are reported to the correct department. Wake-up call sheets (fig. 9-1) are distributed to the switchboard operator, housekeeping, room service, and other departments.

CALL SHEET

Room Number	Call Time, a.m.								
	Before 6:00	6:15	6:30	6:45	7:00	7:15	7:30	7:45	8:00
101					Call				
102							Call		
103			Call						
104	5:30								
105									Call
106			Call						
107								Call	

9-1. Wake-up call sheet.

SPECIAL REQUIREMENTS

It is the responsibility of the front office to pass on to the appropriate department any special requests or requirements of guests. Details of special diets are directed to the executive chef and restaurant manager; a request for an extra bed or cot to be placed in a room would be passed on to the head housekeeper. Any request for valet, laundry, or garage service should be passed to the correct department.

Flowers

Large hotels usually employ a florist on a contractual basis, who regularly supplies and changes the plants and floral arrangements. In smaller establishments the front office or housekeeper may be responsible for the floral decor.

Flowers, plants and their colors can play a significant part if the hotel is asked to organize special functions, such as wedding anniversaries or wedding receptions. For example, when making arrangements for a wedding reception, the front office should ascertain the color schemes chosen by the bride and wedding party and bear that in mind when arranging the floral decor. Details of this nature are important and help create the correct atmosphere.

Wedding anniversaries have tradition and colors associated with them, and these should be borne in mind when organizing such an event; for example:

Wedding Anniversaries	Traditions and Association
First	Cotton
Second	Paper
Third	Leather
Fourth	Flowers
Fifth	Wood
Sixth	Candy
Seventh	Copper
Eighth	Bronze
Ninth	Pottery
Tenth	Tin
Eleventh	Steel
Twelfth	Linen
Thirteenth	Lace
Fourteenth	Ivory
Fifteenth	Crystal
Twentieth	China
Twenty-fifth	Silver
Thirtieth	Pearl
Thirty-fifth	Coral
Fortieth	Ruby
Forty-fifth	Sapphire
Fiftieth	Gold
Fifty-fifth	Emerald
Sixtieth	Diamond

Notable Dates in the Calendar

There are certain very important dates throughout the year which could mean that the hotel is specially decorated or that special functions could be held by various groups or organizations. The front office personnel should be aware of these dates and their associations.

Date	Association
Jan. 1	New Year's Day
Feb. 12	Lincoln's birthday
Feb. 14	Valentine's Day
Feb. 22	Washington's birthday (Obv.)
Feb. 17 (on or about)	Ash Wednesday

Mar. 17	St. Patrick's Day
Mar. (see Jewish calendar)	Purim
Mar. 20	Spring (1st Day)
Mar. 31 (on or about)	Palm Sunday
April 6 (on or about)	Good Friday
April 8 (on or about)	Easter Sunday
April (see Jewish calendar)	Passover
April 23	Secretaries Day
May 17	Armed Forces Day
May 19	Victoria Day
May 26/30	Memorial Day
May 8	Mother's Day
June 19	Father's Day
June 21	Summer (1st Day)
July 4	Independence Day
Sept. 1	Labor Day
Sept. 11	Grandparents Day
Sept. 17	Citizenship Day
Sept. (see Jewish calendar)	Jewish New Year
Sept. 23	Autumn (1st Day)
Oct. (see Jewish calendar)	Rosh Hashana
Oct. (see Jewish calendar)	Yom Kippur
Oct. 12 (Trad.)	Columbus Day
Oct. 24	United Nations Day
Oct. 31	Halloween
Nov. 11	Veterans Day
Nov. (last Thursday in)	Thanksgiving
Dec. 25	Christmas Day
Dec. (see Jewish calendar)	Hanukkah

EMERGENCY FIRST AID

It is in the Rules published by the division that every public food service establishment shall post a sign which illustrates and describes the Heimlich Maneuver procedure for rendering emergency first aid to a choking victim, in a conspicuous place in the establishment accessible to employees.

In case of serious accidents the emergency services must be called immediately, but everyone should have a basic knowledge of first aid and be able to render it when necessary. It should be borne in mind that it is only a temporary measure until the paramedics, doctor, or emergency ambulance service arrives. First aid boxes should be provided and staff shown the contents and where each box is located. When it is necessary to render first aid the basic procedures are listed below.

Bleeding

Direct pressure by either the fingers or hand on an open clean wound will help control the bleeding. Apply a sterile dressing or pad and bandage firmly. Do not apply a tourniquet. If the bleeding is not controlled, increase pressure with the hand and apply more pads. Elevate the bleeding part if possible.

Burns and Scalds

If possible immerse the burn or scald in cold water to alleviate the pain. Do not remove any burnt clothing. Do not apply any oils or ointments, and do not break any blisters. The burnt area should be covered with a dry sterile dressing or some clean fabric. Patients with severe burns should be treated for shock and taken to a hospital or a doctor without delay.

Shock

A person in shock is pale, and the skin usually cold and clammy. The pulse is fast and breathing quick and irregular. The patient should lie down with head low and legs raised slightly. Blankets or clothing should be laid over the patient to keep him or her warm. No stimulants should be given.

Electric Shock

If a patient is still in contact with electrical equipment, switch off the electrical supply at once. If this is not possible, do not touch him or her unless you are protected by rubber gloves or rubber soles on the shoes. Treat as for shock. If the victim is unconscious and the heartbeat or breathing has stopped apply Cardiopulmonary Resuscitation (CPR).

Artificial Respiration and Cardiopulmonary Resuscitation (CPR)

Training for the basic skills of first aid is available everywhere and the most important training is in artificial respiration and cardiopulmonary resuscitation (CPR). Briefly, if a person has ceased to breathe, immediately lay him or her on his or her back. Clear the airways by tilting the head and chin backwards away from the chest. Make sure there is no obstruction by the tongue or foreign matter. Open your mouth, take a deep breath, pinch the patient's nostrils together, then seal his or her mouth with your lips, keeping the head back all the time, and blow into the lungs until the chest rises. Remove your mouth and watch the chest deflate. Give the first four inflations as rapidly as possible, then repeat this operation as long as necessary. Remember time saves lives. CPR involves the application of external heart massage in addition to artificial respiration.

Fainting

Lay the patient down and raise the lower limbs. Loosen tight clothing and ensure fresh air by not allowing people to crowd around the casualty.

The Coma Position

This is sometimes called the *recovery position*. If patients are unconscious but breathing, turn them on their side in a climbing position (one leg slightly bent), so that if they should vomit they will not choke. Dentures should be removed and tight clothing loosened.

Nose Bleed

Sit the patient up with head slightly forward to prevent blood going down the throat and choking him or her. Pinch the fleshy part of the bridge of the nose. If profuse bleeding continues call a doctor.

Foreign Bodies in the Eye

Lifting the upper eyelid over the lower lid will often bring the foreign body on to the lower lid so it can be removed. Blowing the nose will help the eyes to water and wash the object out of the eye. Never rub the eye or use tweezers. If the object is clearly visible, a moistened piece of soft paper can be used to remove it. If the object is embedded in the eyeball, leave it for a doctor to remove. A victim who has a chemical in the eye should not be allowed to rub or close the eyes. Rinse the eye with cold clean water for 15 minutes and take him or her to an emergency room or to a doctor.

Choking

This is usually caused by food or some other foreign body obstructing the windpipe. It can be alleviated by getting the patient to bend forward and with the flat of the hand deliver four hard back blows between the shoulder blades. Then deliver four abdominal thrusts by wrapping your arms around the victim's waist, finding the spot between the breastbone and navel with one hand, and placing the thumb side of the other fist in that spot (NOT over the end of the breastbone). Grasp the fist with your other hand, press the fist in and upwards quickly four times. Repeat back blows and abdominal thrusts.

Poisons

There are Poison Control Centers (PCCs) throughout the country and you should have the emergency number for the center nearest you. Try to find out what kind of poison has been swallowed and call for help. Do not try home remedies until you have been given guidance from the PCC.

Drug Overdose

The major risk in the case of a serious drug overdose is that the patient may vomit and choke, or lose consciousness and stop breathing. If the victim is unconscious turn him or her onto the coma position on his or her side to prevent vomit or fluids entering the airways or lungs. Remove any dentures and loosen tight clothing. If the patient stops breathing, render artificial respiration to keep the oxygen going to the brain. Call for emergency help and try to find the container of the drugs swallowed; it will help the doctor.

Fractures

Move the patient as little as possible. Immobilize and support the injured part. Call an ambulance. Treat for shock if necessary.

Convulsions

A person suffering a convulsion usually falls to the ground, becomes rigid, and has a seizure. It is important that the victim is prevented from doing any self-harm. Try to separate the victim's teeth, then place something safe in the mouth to bite on; do not use force. Stay with the victim until the seizure is over. Turn the victim over onto his or her side. Call an ambulance.

ACCIDENTS

The division lays down in its rules and regulations the minimum acceptable standards of safety and welfare. Beyond adhering to the set standards, the hotel should take reasonable care and precautions to prevent likely harm or injury to staff or guests. Staff should be made aware of the common causes of accidents. If they notice anything that could prove hazardous, they should report it immediately so that it can be remedied.

Accident-Prevention Precautions

The most common accidents in public places occur because the following precautions have not been taken:

- Carpets should be secure and tight, stair carpet in particular. Any cuts or tears should be repaired.
- Floors should be kept in good repair, and notices posted indicating wet or polished floors that could be hazardous.
- Any low doorways, projections, or unexpected steps should be clearly marked.
- Passageways should be well lit.
- All equipment should be well maintained.

Accident Book

When an accident, however minor, does occur, it should be recorded in an accident book. Full details should be given: the names and addresses of those concerned, an account of the accident, and names and addresses of any witnesses. This report should be made immediately, while the details are fresh in mind.

FIRE SAFETY

Instructions for action in case of fire should be prominently displayed in all rooms. Exits should be clearly marked and access to them kept clear and unblocked. All staff should know where fire-fighting equipment is located and what action must be taken in the case of fire or any other such emergency. If fire breaks out, the staff must assist switchboard operators in notifying all guests in the danger areas to vacate.

Emergency Procedures

1. In case of fire, the automatic sprinkler, smoke detector and fire alarm system will alert the staff, and the fire department will be called.
2. Staff must only undertake fire-fighting if they have been trained.
3. Hotel employees will assist all elderly, sick, or disabled people to exits.
4. The front office staff should, if possible, collect the register, and lists of residents and staff, and take them from the building in order that all persons can be accounted for.
5. When the building has been cleared, staff and guests should be assembled away from the area and be checked.
6. Staff should stay calm and make every effort to calm the guests and get them clear of the building.

SECURITY PRECAUTIONS

A hotel presents many problems of security. It is almost impossible to safeguard the property and premises completely even with security guards and sophisticated security systems. Closed circuit television (CCTV) monitoring passages and security officers in public rooms are part of most large hotels, but common-sense precautions will also help in crime prevention.

Guests' Property

Security precautions for the care of guests' property include:

1. Broken door locks should be repaired immediately.
2. Guests should be encouraged not to leave valuables lying around the room. The maid should report any laxity to the housekeeper, who can then advise the guest on safer keeping.

3. The maid service must scrupulously lock room doors after cleaning. If rooms are on the ground floor, windows should be closed and locked when the rooms are empty.
4. All property found in rooms or elsewhere should be handed to the head housekeeper who will see it is entered in the lost and found book and placed in safekeeping.

Security of Premises

The need for security varies greatly according to the size and location of the hotel. These are a few of the most basic, routine security measures that should be taken, but all personnel should be aware of the need for vigilance and security precautions at all times.

• Staff must quickly familiarize themselves with the guests and other members of staff, and be instructed to question anyone on the premises that they are not familiar with or whom they consider may be acting in a suspicious manner.
• Security checks should be made on the building at regular intervals.
• Keys and master keys must be kept under strict supervision at all times.
• Monies and valuables on the premises should be locked away, or kept under strict surveillance at all times while being handled in the course of business.

CHAPTER SUMMARY

This chapter deals with the importance of the front office as a communication center working in cooperation with all departments.
Points and topics discussed are:

• The work of the housekeeping department
• The linen room
• The responsibility of the front office to pass on to the appropriate department any special requests made by the guest
• The association of colors, flowers and plants for decor and special events
• Notable dates on the calendar and their significance
• Emergency situations that could arise requiring a basic knowledge of first aid

- Accidents in the hotel
- Action in the case of fire
- Security precautions

FOR DISCUSSION

1. Discuss the role of the head housekeeper and the importance of good communication between the housekeeping department and the front office.
2. Discuss the type of situation which could arise in a hotel making it necesssary for a member of staff to render first aid as a temporary measure while awaiting the emergency services.
3. Discuss the importance of the accident book and why it is essential that all members of the staff be alert and report immediately anything that could prove hazardous or cause an accident to either a guest or other members of the staff.
4. What are the correct procedures to follow in the case of fire?
5. With the continual flow of traffic through a hotel/motel security is difficult to maintain. How can staff members help safeguard the hotel and guests against intruders and anyone behaving in a suspicious manner?

KEY TERMS

Ancillary duties
Bed occupancy and room availability reports
Emergency first aid
Safety regulations and security precautions

CHAPTER QUIZ

1. Explain the importance of close liaison between the housekeeping, other departments, and the front office.

2. What floral or special decorations would you suggest for guests who were celebrating the following wedding anniversaries:
   a. Seventh
   b. Fifteenth

c. Twenty-fifth
d. Thirty-fifth
e. Fortieth
f. Fiftieth

3. Describe briefly the initial action you would take in the following circumstances:
   a. A guest receives a minor burn on the hand.
   b. A lady falls down in a faint at the reception desk.
   c. An electrician working on repairs receives a mild electric shock.
   d. A guest starts choking on a piece of food in the restaurant.

4. The hotel has to be evacuated because of fire. What action should be taken by the staff? What information should the front office staff try to rescue to pass on to the fire officer in charge?

5. A very agitated guest reports at the front desk that a valuable watch is missing from her room. What action would the desk clerk take?

6. Special functions have been booked on the following dates:

   February 14
   March 17
   July 4
   October 31

   What do you associate with these dates? Recommend what colors, plants, or floral decoration you would incorporate in the arrangements.

FACTS AND FIGURES
OF TOURISM

The Department of Commerce, Division of Economic Development, and Bureau of Economic Analysis of many states regularly publish facts and figures on the impact of tourism on their state's economy. These statistics prove invaluable to those engaged in market research and analysis for the hotel industry.

Typical of these facts and figures are those published by the state of Florida, where tourism has a very positive impact ranging from increased employment to a reduction in tax for the residents.

What follows is a sampling provided by the Florida Department of Commerce showing the estimated data for visitor arrivals to Florida from 1977 to 1985.

VISITOR ARRIVALS: AUTO AND AIR

When studying the data from the tourist industry, the time factor must be taken into consideration. The figures for a given year are not available until the following year; nevertheless, market researchers study trends and forecast the probable direction the industry will take.

Total Estimated Visitors Arrivals
1977–1985

Year	Visitors	Year	Visitors
1977	18,748,598	1982	27,017,984
1978	21,514,232	1983	28,923,833
1979	23,693,652	1984	30,151,485
1980	24,686,348	1985	32,217,205
1981	25,018,132		

Source: Florida Department of Commerce

The estimated arrivals to Florida from 1977 to 1985 show an average yearly increase of 7.1 percent. This total includes auto, domestic air, and international visitors.

International Air Tourist Arrivals

Year	Visitors
1977	786,000
1978	1,003,860
1979	1,500,000
1980	2,100,000
1981	3,000,000
1982	2,772,747
1983	2,400,000
1984	2,000,000
1985	2,100,000

Source: Florida Department of Commerce, Division of Tourism, Office of Marketing Research

SEASONAL FACTORS

The tourism industry has seasonal variations. The Hotel & Motel Association in Florida and other states provide the Bureau of Economic Analysis with monthly occupancy rates, for example:

(Percentage of Rooms Sold)	
1985	
January	53.1
February	70.3
March	81.0
April	72.2
May	64.2
June	64.2
July	66.3
August	62.1
September	47.2
October	55.6
November	55.7
December	50.5

Source: Florida Hotel & Motel Association, 1985

The highest occupancy rates are February, March, and April, the lowest in September. This decrease corresponded with the decrease in estimated auto visitors arriving in September.

APPENDIX B

HOTEL INDUSTRY ASSOCIATIONS

Addresses for the following associations can be found in trade magazines such as *Hotel Motel Management, Lodging Hospitality Magazine*, and *Meeting News*.

American Hotel & Motel Association (AH & MA)
American Society of Association Executives (ASAE)
American Society for Training and Development (ASTD)
American Society of Travel Agents (ASTA)
Association of National Tourist Office Reps
Convention Liaison Council of Engineering & Scientific Society Executives (CESSE)
Exhibit Designers & Producers Association (ED & PA)
Exposition Service Contractors Association (ESCA)
Health Care Exhibitors Association (HCEA)
Hotel Sales & Marketing Association (HSMAI)
Institute of Association Management Companies (IAMC)
Insurance Conference Planners Association (ICPA)
International Association of Auditorium Managers (IAAM)
International Association of Conference Centers (IACC)
International Association of Convention & Visitors Bureaus (IACVB)
International Association of Fairs and Expositions (IAFE)
International Exhibitors Association (IEA)

International Hotel Association
Meeting Planners International (MPI)
National Association of Exposition Managers (NAEM)
National Passenger Traffic Association (NPTA)
Professional Convention Management Association (PCMA)
Religious Conference Management Association (RCMA)
Sales and Marketing Executives International (SMEI)
Society of Company Meeting Planners (SCMP)
Society of Incentive Travel Executives (SITE)
Travel Industry Association of America
Washington Society of Association Executives
Western Society of Association Executives (WSAE)

APPENDIX C

THE TELEPHONE ALPHABET

Clear enunciation is important when having to spell words over the telephone; therefore, a system of analogy should be used. For example:

A	as in Andrew	N	as in Nellie
B	Benjamin	O	Olive
C	Charlie	P	Peter
D	David	Q	Queenie
E	Edward	R	Robert
F	Father	S	Sugar
G	George	T	Tommy
H	Harry	U	Uncle
I	Isaac	V	Victor
J	Jack	W	William
K	Kenneth	X	Xmas
L	Lucy	Y	Yellow
M	Mother	Z	Zebra

THE METRIC SYSTEM

The metric system is a decimal system which was devised by the French after the revolution in 1789 in an attempt to rationalize their counting methods. The Systems Internationale (SI) is now used for every aspect of life which is measured, from cosmic rays to medicine to cooking ingredients.

The system is simple; each denomination is one tenth of the one above it and ten times the one below it.

The gram is the unit of weight

1 kilogram (kg) = 1000 grams (or 10 hg)
1 hectogram (hg) = 100 grams (or 10 dag)
1 decagram (dag) = 10 grams (1/10 or 0.1 gram)
1 centigram (cg) = 1/100 or 0.01 gram
1 milligram (mg) = 1/1000 or 0.001 gram

The meter is the unit of length

1 kilometer (km) = 1000 meters (or 10 hm)
1 hectameter (hm) = 100 meters (or 10 dam)
1 decameter (dam) = 10 meters
1 decimeter (dm) = 1/10 or 0.1 meter
1 centimeter (cm) = 1/100 or 0.01 meter
1 millimeter (mm) = 1/1000 or 0.001 meter

The liter is the unit of capacity

1 kiloliter (kl) = 1000 liters (or 10 hl)
1 hectoliter (hl) = 100 liters (or 10 dl)
1 decaliter (dal) = 10 liters
1 deciliter (dl) = 1/10 or 0.1 liter
1 centiliter (cl) = 1/100 or 0.01 liter
1 milliliter (ml) = 1/1000 or 0.001 liter

USEFUL EQUIVALENTS

1 pint = 0.473 liters
1 gallon = 3.8 liters
1 inch = 25.4 millimeters
1 foot = 0.3 meters
1 mile = 1.609 kilometers
1 ounce = 28.4 grams
1 pound = 0.5 kilograms

Index

Debit, 101, 113
Debit note, 106-107
Defraud, intent to, 182
Delivery ticket, 104
Density chart, 44
Departed guests, mail for, 139
Department of Commerce, Division
    of Tourism, 162
Departures, procedures for, 68-69
Deposits, 53, 123
Diplomacy, 19-21
Direct inward dialing (DID), 79
Discounted rate, 31
Discounts, special, 54
"Division," 58, 175, 176
Division of Hotels and Restaurants,
    Department of Business Regula-
    tion. *See* "Division"
Do not disturb request, 79
Dot matrix printer, 147
Double-entry bookkeeping, 99-101
Drinking, after hours, 183-184
Drug overdose, 196

Early departure, 54
Eight hundred (800) toll-free service,
    77
Electric shock, 194
Electronic key system, 63-64
Electronic laser printer, 147
Electronic room status boards,
    47, 78
Electronic typewriters, 146-147
Emergency first aid, 193-197
Emergency interrupt line, 78
Emergency numbers, 77
Employers' Tax Guide (Dept. of
    Labor), 152, 153
En bloc booking, 57-58
England, 1
Equal Employment Opportunity
    Commission (EEOC),
    184-185
Equal Pay Act (EPA), 185
Equivalents, measurement, 212
Establishment rules, 180
Executive room, 7
Express mail services, 142
External subsystems, 129
Eye, foreign bodies in, 195-196

Facsimile (FAX) communication,
    80
Fainting, 195
Fair Labor Standards Act (FLSA),
    185
Fatalities, 183
Filing, 143-145
Fire Marshall rules, 178-179
Fire safety, 198
First aid, 193-197
Floppy disk, 127
Flowers, 191
Folder inserter, 147-148
Forecasting, 165-167
Foreign currencies, 126
Foreign Tourist Bureau, 96
Foreign visitors, pecentage of,
    163
Form 4070, 153
Fractures, 197
Franchise system, 2-3
Front office
    bell captain's desk, 11
    billing office, 10
    cashier's office, 10
    evening duties, 71
    function of, 8-9
    housekeeping department, 11
    information desk, 10
    manager, 9-10
    morning duties, 70-71
    sales department function, 85
Future guests, mail for, 139

Giveaways, 93, 95
Gram, 211
Graphs, 164-165
Great Depression, 2
Group registration, 55-56, 130
Groups, 90-92
    arrival of, 56-57
    booking form, 55
    departure of, 57
Guaranteed arrival, 53-54
Guaranteed reservations, 48, 52
Guests
    accounting applications, 131
    definition of, 175
    history card, 73
    mail for, 139